WATERWAY WALKS IN LEICESTERSHIRE and RUTLAND

Paul Biggs

Published by Sigma Leisure – an imprint of
Sigma Press, 1 South Oak Lane, Wilmslow, Cheshire SK9 6AR, England.

British Library Cataloguing in Publication Data
A CIP record for this book is available from the British Library.

ISBN: 1-85058-442-7

Reprinted: 1999

Typesetting and Design by: Sigma Press, Wilmslow, Cheshire.

Cover photograph: the author climbing a stile on the River Soar footpath. Opposite is Normanton-on-Soar church. *(Sandy Biggs)*

Text Photographs: Paul Biggs

Maps: Jeremy Semmens

Printed by: MFP Design & Print

PREFACE

Over the last decade I have walked many miles in Leicestershire and this has made me aware that my adopted county is far more attractive than I realised. Whether it is with my young family for an afternoon's stroll or a strenuous day's walking with my faithful dog Ben, I am constantly reminded that it is worthwhile examining what is on your own doorstep rather than dashing along the motorway in search of Utopia.

A cursory inspection of a map of Leicestershire will reveal that the county is naturally divided into two unequal halves with the River Soar and the Grand Union Canal loosely forming the boundary line. In the west, the rocky outcrops of Charnwood Forest and the hustle and bustle of city life contrast sharply against the east, with the lonely hills of High Leicestershire and the sedate pace of life in the quaint market towns. Whatever your preference, and my allegiances lie with the west, this heart of the shires county has it all and you will not be disappointed in any area you choose to walk.

"What makes a good walk?" is a question that I am often asked and the answer is simple. Plan your route carefully, ensuring that the length of the walk is well within your capabilities. There is nothing more tedious than slogging over the last few miles and spoiling what perhaps would have been an enjoyable day out. Never hurry a walk, as you may miss many hidden delights in attempting to complete the circuit in the shortest possible time. A walk can be compared to a good wine – linger over its qualities, enjoy the freshness, and above all take time in its completion.

I have always had an affinity for walking by water and this book has given me the opportunity to assemble 30 magical walks throughout Leicestershire and Rutland that will transport you back in time. Waterways hold many pleasures and treasures and without doubt there is something for everyone to discover.

My thanks are extended to my wife Sandra, for without her patience and understanding this book would not have been possible. I must also thank my two young sons, Danny and Tommy, as I know that they have missed their Dad at weekends while he has been out researching the walks. Also, a mention for the following people: Trudie Colotto, Rick Colotto, Ginny Copley, and John Cooper who have all helped in their different ways. Lastly, thanks to Lynn Roe for her hard work in reading my notes and typing the manuscript.

Paul Biggs

Contents

INTRODUCTION

THE WALKS

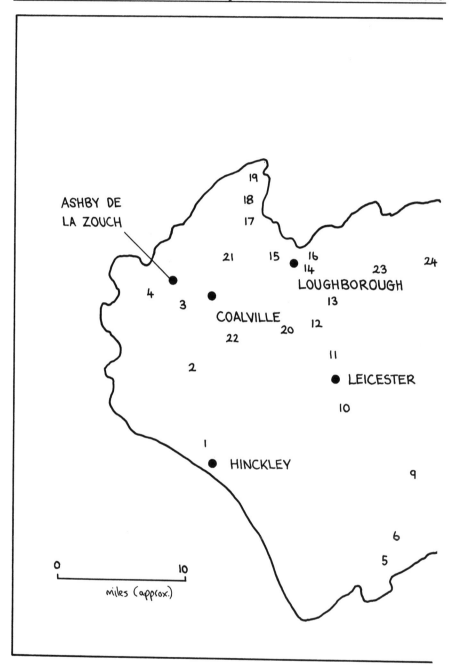

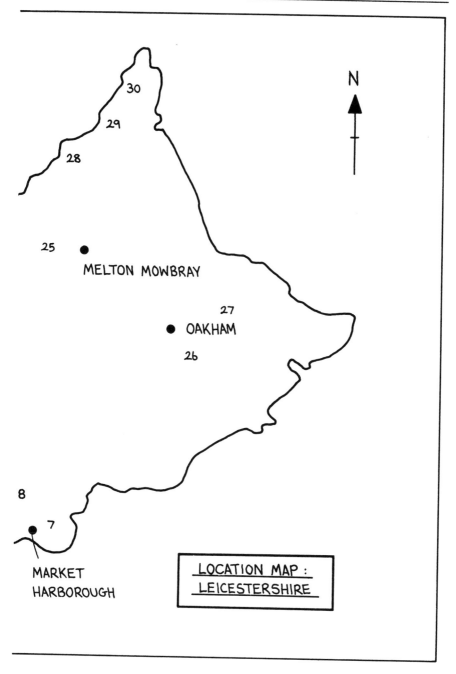

INTRODUCTION

This book contains 30 walks, 28 of which are circular, between three and ten miles which will suit all the family. If every walk were to be completed then a grand total of over 180 miles would be clocked up. But this book is not about "clocking up miles" and for that reason most of the walks fall into the four to eight mile category. If desired several of the shorter walks could easily be linked together to offer a wider choice of longer walks that should appeal to the more serious-minded walker.

The Joy of Walking

Walking is considered by many to be one our most popular pastimes and it is also healthy for us. I agree, and even on the bleakest of days, provided you are wrapped in warm clothing, a walk through the unkindest of elements can be turned into a happy occasion. With our seasons being so varied and interesting, all of these walks should be tried at any time of the year for optimum enjoyment. The arrival of winter does not signal the end of the walking season and the putting away of those boots.

Walking boots or stout shoes are essential as riverside paths, field footpaths, bridleways, and tracks are liable to be wet and slippy from inclement weather or generally uneven. The greater protection against losing your footing, or perhaps a twisted ankle, the better. There are plenty of reasonably-priced boots on the market to choose from and trainers or slip-on shoes are unsuitable for even the shortest of countryside strolls.

Make sure that you always carry a map. I find that a map case with the relevant part of the exposed map showing through the clear plastic front, hung around the neck, is most useful. The map case can be lifted up to eye level to check the route, and also gives further information of the surrounding area. This saves much searching through pockets or rucksack looking for the map itself, then further time opening it out to find the section of the walk. On a breezy day the map case is not so good as the string attachment twists quickly, and catches you unawares, twisting tightly around your neck. A gentle hand placed on the case as you walk along will overcome this problem. Returning to maps the O.S. Landranger 1:50000 series general purpose maps give a reasonable amount of detail including roads, railways, tourist information, general features, and heights. Rights of Way are shown as short and long red dashes. These are adequate for most people but the O.S. Pathfinder 1:25000 series covers a smaller local area and are particularly good if you are following a path for the first time as they indicate where the path extends over the field or through the wood for instance. Similar features to the Landranger series are shown but Rights of Way are denoted by green dashes.

What do you look for when out walking? Water, landscape views, pretty villages, old pubs, quaint churches perhaps. If so, then your idea of walking and mine are very alike. I have endeavoured to include each of these components in almost every walk and I am grateful to the county for being so rich in historic wealth and making my task of selecting these walks so much easier.

Ashby Canal

The Ashby Canal, or Ashby de la Zouch Canal as it is sometimes known, stretches from Marston Junction, near Bedworth to just north of Snarestone, a distance of 21¾ miles, being completely lock-free. A continuous tow path runs the length of the canal and is available for public use, although some sections are not Rights of Way; they may be closed by British Waterways at any time if necessary. There are limited facilities for the disabled with wheelchair access available at certain points.

Originally it was intended that the Ashby Canal would be a through route to the River Trent from the Coventry Canal. In 1792 an Ashby Canal Company was formed and a year later presented a Bill to Parliament which was passed in 1794. The Act allowed for a broad canal from Marston to the Ashby Wolds coalfields and followed the 300 foot contour line for 30 miles. The section north of Moira was found to be very expensive and was never constructed, while tramways were built to link the various coalfields and limeworks. By 1804 the canal was opened throughout at a total cost of £184,000.

In 1846 the Midland Railway bought the Ashby Canal much to the dismay of Oxford and Coventry canal companies as they stood to lose revenue if coal was switched from canal to rail, which in the end did not happen. In 1918 a major breach of the canal occurred at Moira, and although repaired, further subsidence in the Measham area from the coalfields plagued the canal. During the early 1940s the new owners of the canal, the London, Midland, and Scottish Railway offered the canal free of charge to the Coventry Canal Company, to get it off their hands, but the offer was spurned. By 1966, nine miles of the canal had been abandoned resulting in the current terminal about one mile north of Snarestone.

Future prospects look good for the canal with the Measham Canal Restoration Group investigating the prospects of restoring the abandoned canal north of Snarestone with the possibility of re-opening the canal to the original terminus.

The Grand Union Canal

The Grand Union Canal begins at Little Venice in London and works it way northwards to Birmingham with a branch line at Norton Junction near Daventry that extends to Leicester (Leicester Line) and Loughborough (Soar Navigation). There are two 'Arms' off the Leicester Line, one reaches Welford while the other stretches to Market Harborough.

In 1778, the Soar Navigation opened the Loughborough canal which gave boats access from Loughborough to the River Trent via the River Soar, bringing immediate prosperity to the town. This was mainly due to the close proximity of the Nottinghamshire and Derbyshire coalfields and the Erewash Canal. An Act was passed in 1791 for the extension of the Soar Navigation to Leicester and the Leicester canal was opened on 21st February 1794.

With the need to transport coal to London construction work began in 1793 in Leicester to take the canal southwards but owing to financial problems the canal was terminated at Debdale Wharf in 1797. 12 years later it was continued to Foxton and Market Harborough, opening in 1809, and by 1814 the final stage from Foxton to Norton Junction was completed joining the London to Birmingham Grand Union Canal.

Today, the canal is extremely popular with pleasure boats, while a tow path runs parallel to the waterway offering many recreational pursuits. A small amount of local freight is still carried. In 1994 a canal barge was used to transport five church bells along the Grand Union Canal from Marsworth near Tring to Loughborough basin for restoration at John Taylor Bell Founders Ltd. The journey took 11 days with the bells returning in the same manner. It is believed that it was the first time this century that bells have been taken to and from Loughborough by canal. It was a fitting tribute to the bicentenary of the waterway.

River Soar

Approximately 40 miles long, the River Soar rises at Smockington Hollow on the Warwickshire border and begins life as the Soar Brook. At Sharnford it becomes the River Soar, but in truth is no more than a wide stream, until it passes beneath the M1 Motorway near to Narborough, to join the Grand Union Canal close to Aylestone, Leicester. From the City to the Trent the River Soar forms the Soar Navigation, encompassing the Leicester Navigation and Loughborough Navigation.

In 1634 Thomas Skipworth of Cotes was granted a licence from King Charles I to make the river navigable to Leicester and was awarded a sum of money for this venture. In return 10% of all profit was to be given to the King, but the scheme failed.

With the arrival of the Loughborough and Leicester canals the River Soar became navigable and prospered until the coming of the Midland Counties Railway to Leicester in 1840. However, the navigations struggled on despite fierce competition from the railways until 1932 when they were both bought by the Grand Union in an attempt to 'beef up' traffic and unify the canal. An upsurge in traffic resulted, but this proved temporary and by 1948 when the waterways were nationalised, the battle for commercial business was all but lost.

A rosy future lies ahead for the river with its popularity increasing year by year. Pleasure craft and boating holidays offer a unique chance to explore the tranquil countryside in the Soar Valley, canoeing, while angling and riverside walking are favourite pastimes. In fact it is possible to walk from Leicester West Bridge to the River Trent, a distance of 25 miles, by using the riverside tow path and public footpaths. Why not try this one summer weekend spending a night at a bed and breakfast establishment in one of the many villages by the Soar. Transport will need to be arranged at Red Hill Lock to return you to your starting point or to Loughborough where a bus or train can be taken to Leicester.

River Wreake

The River Wreake is a tributary of the Soar, joining the river and canal system north of Syston. Covering 15 miles to Melton Mowbray the river passes through the delightful Wreake Valley countryside. It is a perfect example of a natural river, moulded by man, and dates back to pre-Saxon time.

The word 'Wreake' comes from the Scandinavian name 'twisting' which more than describes the course of the short river. In 1794 the river was made navigable with numerous twists of the waterway being straightened to allow the Wreake Navigation to open. From Melton Mowbray the Oakham Canal extended the navigation to Oakham.

With the advent of the railways the demise of the Oakham canal happened quickly and in 1846 the canal closed. The Wreake Navigation continued for a further 30 years, finally closing to traffic in 1876.

Each village along the Wreake had a watermill for the grinding of corn and the manufacture of flour for bread; walking by the river today, you will see that many of these fine buildings have been restored to beautiful residences. The river is not navigable, but it provides an excellent habitat for flora and fauna. It is not possible to walk the length of the Wreake, but many public footpaths follow the riverside linking together the villages in the valley.

The Grantham Canal

The Grantham Canal passes through three counties: Nottinghamshire, Leicestershire, and Lincolnshire travelling 33 miles from the River Trent, Nottingham to Grantham. The canal falls 139 feet nine inches, between the two terminal points, by means of 18 locks. However, these will no longer be found, as the canal was abandoned in 1936 and the locks removed.

In 1793 an Act of Parliament was approved for the canal and work commenced immediately. Four years later in 1797, the canal was opened wholly at a cost of £118,500 and apart from the Erewash

Canal it was the cheapest per mile of the East Midlands canals to construct. The canal made a reasonable profit during the first half of the nineteenth century with coal and coke being the main commodities carried. 1850 saw the opening of the Nottingham to Grantham railway line and the Grantham Canal Company were willing to merge with the railway. It was four years later when finally the Ambergate Company bought the canal and after many railway amalgamations ownership passed to the L.N.E.R. Gradually traffic dwindled and after a period of inactivity the canal was abandoned.

Today the canal is maintained by British Waterways and a tow path (permissive) runs parallel to the water for much of its length. The disused canal meanders through exceptionally pretty countryside especially in the Vale of Belvoir. The Grantham Canal Restoration Society is working extremely hard to restore the canal back to its former glory and their object is to see the canal navigable again.

Public Transport

Leicestershire is well-served by trains and buses with all of the major towns in the county having a railway station. Fairly frequent train services connect the towns being operated either by InterCity or Regional Railways. I have ensured that all walks may be reached by public transport, albeit that one or two starting points may have to be altered to coincide with the bus route, but alternative details are given within the appropriate section of the walk.

Basic bus service detail has been included, but since deregulation bus operators are free to come and go virtually overnight and it is essential that times and services are checked beforehand. Busline has information on all bus services in Leicestershire and Rutland being provided by the Public Transport Unit at County Hall, Glenfield, Leicester. The telephone service is sponsored by all of the local authorities in the county, who are helpful even with the most difficult enquiry. They are also willing to post a bus timetable of the area that you wish to visit to you, telephone them on 0116 251 1411.

Geography

The River Soar and Grand Union Canal run from North-West to South-East through Leicestershire and make a natural East/West division of the county. East Leicestershire is referred to as "High

Leicestershire" since much of the countryside is in the region of 600 feet above sea level with the iron age escarpment of Burrough Hill standing over 700 feet and well-known to walkers. It forms part of the Stone Belt which crosses England from Dorset to the Yorkshire Coast.

West Leicestershire has the rocky outcrops of Charnwood, named after Charnwood Forest, and Bardon Hill at 912 feet is the highest point in Leicestershire. Charnwood Forest no longer exists but this small area of Charnwood contains volcanic rock formations from 700 million years ago when volcanoes erupted and deposited ash to form these rocks in pre-Cambrian times. Further south, within Charnwood, is Bradgate Park. If you ever wondered how a medieval deer park looked, then a walk through the 850 acre natural park will enlighten and enchant you.

The north west has adopted the name "Ivanhoe Country" after Sir Walter Scott's novel 'Ivanhoe' as this typifies the area. The region is mainly farming with the renown Leicestershire coalfields around Coalville now becoming redundant leaving Open Cast mining in the Ashby de la Zouch vicinity. Ivanhoe County is soon to take on a new guise being at the heart of the National Forest, the most significant development of its kind this century. The former coal-pit at Moira has been chosen to become the Visitors Centre for the Forest which will bring increased tourism to this part of the county.

Harborough District covers much of the south west, extending some 230 square miles from the A5 road border with Warwickshire to Rutland in the east, while to the south is the county boundary of Northamptonshire. The area is noted for rolling hills and tranquillity, but has excellent road communications especially to Market Harborough with a junction provided for the town from the new A1/M1 link road.

The north east falls into two parts, the steep clay and limestone sloping ridge that overlooks the Vale of Belvoir terminating by Belvoir Castle, and the valley of the Rivers Wreake and Eye that runs east to west passing through the centre of Melton Mowbray. Burrough Hill, a few miles south of Melton Mowbray, is an old iron age hill fort dating back from about 800 BC and probably occupied for about 600 years.

In the south east, lies tiny Rutland, an area of 15 miles long and 15 miles wide. Within the locality is Rutland Water, a gigantic reservoir, built in the 1970s to quench the demand for water in neighbouring towns. Rutland is so traditionally English, where time appears to standstill. The feel-good factor that is missing so much in other areas of the country is very definitely evident here.

Local Traditions

Leicestershire is a county long associated with hunting, cheese, and pork pies. There has always been some form of hunting in Leicestershire and Rutland ever since the Middle Ages, but today the county is looked upon for being the home of the most famous fox hunting packs in England. In all six packs regularly meet and the county is divided up as follows: The Quorn hunts over the north, while The Fernie covers the south, The Belvoir meets in the north east, with The Cottesmore found in the neighbouring east. The West of Leicestershire sees The Atherstone which leaves The Pytchley, predominantly a Northamptonshire pack, meeting on occasions in the extreme south. Whatever your views on fox hunting as a sport, it has to be accepted that "The Hunt" has been responsible for retaining the status quo in our fields with many hedges saved from today's modern farming methods.

Stilton cheese has been produced in Leicestershire for over 300 years, being named after a village on the old Great North Road now in Cambridgeshire. Why should such a Leicestershire cheese bear the name of a village from another county? The answer is simple, in about 1720 Mrs Orton of Little Dalby made a creamy white cheese and supplied this to the landlord of the Bell Inn, Stilton who sold it to travellers calling at the Coaching Inn. However, the cheese was made years earlier and was known as Quenby cheese. All Mrs Orton did was to perfect and sell the cheese to her brother-in-law at the pub. Once popular, dairies in Leicestershire saw that there was a ready market and exploited it to its fullest. Today there are six firms in Leicestershire manufacturing the blue veined and white cheese, selling world-wide. Red Leicester cheese is also produced in the county stretching back to the eighteenth century with its origins firmly in the south. Nowadays, Red Leicester is sold in supermarkets in vacuum-packed blocks being made in Melton Mowbray and Harby.

Melton Mowbray is the home for pork pie making. It was as long ago as 1831 when Edward Adcock first produced pork pies in a small baker's shop on Leicester Street. By 1840 a pork pie factory was in full swing started by Enoch Evans and pork pies quickly became a favourite with the hunting fraternity. Today Dickinson and Morris are the only firm in Melton Mowbray producing pork pies. Their shop on Nottingham Street sells the traditional pie along with The Original Melton Hunt Cake, a rich quality fruit cake, made to their own patented recipe since 1854.

Walk 1: Stoke Golding and the Ashby Canal

Distance: 5½ miles

Maps: O.S. Landranger 140, Leicester and Coventry area; O.S. Pathfinder 914 (SP29/39)

Location: Stoke Golding is 2½ miles from Hinckley located off the A447 road. Start from the George and Dragon public house in the village centre. Grid reference 398972.

Parking: Small area outside the post office otherwise park on the road side around pub.

Refreshments: George and Dragon and Three Horseshoes, Stoke Golding – both recommended. Canal shop at Stoke Golding wharf. The Fox Inn, Higham on the Hill.

Public Transport:

By Rail: Nearest British Rail station is at Hinckley

By Bus: Nuneaton/Hinckley fairly frequent service operated by Midland Fox.

Stoke Golding and Higham on the Hill are two classy villages overlooking the Ashby Canal situated on opposite banks. This figure of eight walk links both villages and is designed to be taken at a sedate pace to drink in the interesting rural countryside views and varied canal aquatic wildlife on offer. A choice of three pubs in Stoke Golding all serve excellent refreshments. If walking with a young family, children are made most welcome at the Three Horseshoes.

The Route

Not everyone will be aware that as you walk along the Ashby canal tow path from Stoke Golding just a few miles to the west is the centre of England – the furthest point from the sea. There is no actual landmark as it appears that not all the relevant bodies are in agreement with regards to the precise location of the Centre of England.

A busy boating scene on the Ashby Canal at Stoke Golding wharf

From the George and Dragon, turn onto High Street passing the Three Horseshoes pub and follow the road round to the left. Pass the Parish Church of St Margaret, then the White Swan pub to a public footpath sign on the left at the end of the village. From the stile a short field path leads to bridge 27 over the Ashby Canal. Cross over the bridge, join the tow path on your left and walk to the right noting the fine spire of Stoke Golding church away to the left.

Cross a new bridge over a water inlet that feeds the Ashby Canal Centre, which offers a professional service for the boat owner, and is of fairly recent construction. Pass beneath bridge 26 enjoying the rural country scenes on offer and in a ¼ mile Stoke Golding Wharf is reached where the Ashby Boat Company have their headquarters. Narrow boats may be hired here for the day or week for a relaxing cruise along the beautiful winding canal. At bridge 23 an Ashby Canal signpost is passed indicating that Hinckley Wharf is 2½ miles along the Ambion Way. In fact the tow path forms about half of the eight mile circular walk from Hinckley to Sutton Wharf (Sutton Cheney) and this walk takes in the majority of the canal section. Continue along the tow path passing the new moorings at Wykin and if you are lucky you may spot the beautiful blue plumage of a kingfisher flying along the canal bank.

Just prior to reaching bridge 20 leave the tow path at a public footpath sign for Higham on the Hill one mile and climb a stile that leads into a field. Cross to a marker post opposite then climb a fence onto the old track bed of the Ashby and Nuneaton Joint Railway. The branch from Hinckley to Ashby joined the Nuneaton route just south of Stoke Golding and both lines opened simultaneously in 1873. The Hinckley branch line was dismantled in 1900 having never carried a fare paying passenger. From the next stile a field perimeter path is followed to a market post, then a vague path cuts diagonally right to a well-hidden footbridge in a hedge. Keep a hedge close to your left on the field perimeter path and continue ahead in the same direction crossing a series of stiles to reach the road at Higham on the Hill.

Walk along the road through the village then turn right at a road junction to reach a footpath sign after about ¼ mile. A short detour may be taken into the main part of the village of Higham on the Hill as this walk misses the better parts of the village. Follow the hedge to the left to a gate, then turn right over a stile to join an obvious field path ahead to a stile in the far corner. Continue ahead over the

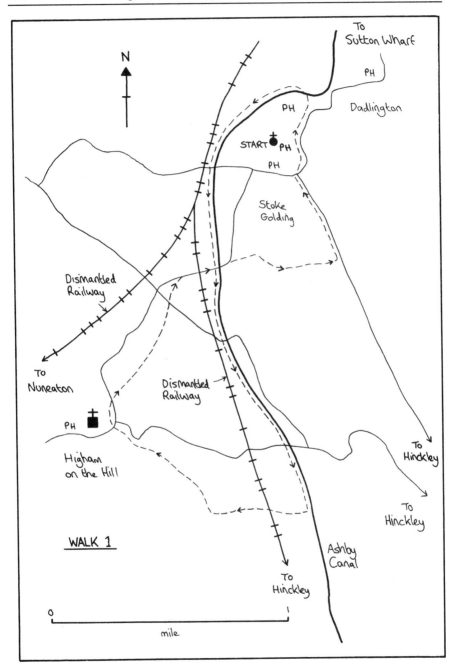

next field path to reach a stile and the road. Turn left for 75 yards to a public footpath sign on the right where an awkward stile and fence gives access to a diagonal field path to the left. Turn right along the road crossing over the dismantled railway line, then the Ashby Canal to a footpath sign on the right.

Go through the gate onto a rough track that climbs slowly towards Millfield Farm then bear left onto a obvious field path with a hedge adjacent to your left. Continue ahead over two more fields to eventually reach the road. Turn left and walk along the road for about ¼ mile back into Stoke Golding and the George and Dragon.

Points of Interest

Stoke Golding has a beautiful and dignified village church that was built between 1290 and 1340. St Margaret's church is well worth visiting to inspect the delicate tracery of its windows and arcade. Nearby is Crown Hill where Henry Tudor was crowned king after the Battle of Bosworth Field in August 1485.

Dadlington is a tiny village built around the village green with an enchanting inn called the Dog and Hedgehog. It has a superb reputation for succulent porterhouse steaks. The small church of St James dates back to the thirteenth century but was extensively restored in the late nineteenth century. In the nave and south aisle the original timbers survive in the roof and the church claims connections with the Bosworth Battlefield where many soldiers were killed and a number are allegedly buried in the churchyard.

Higham on the Hill as the name implies stands on a hill overlooking the Ashby Canal with views of rural South West Leicestershire. St Peter's church has the only complete Norman tower in South Leicestershire and has a fine peal of bells with one bell, the Armada bell, cast in 1589. There are two pubs, the Fox Inn and the Oddfellows Arms, both serving food and are welcome hostelries to walkers.

Footnote

This is a very pleasant walk along the canal, where the aquatic wildlife is of particular interest. Fish such as carp, tench and pike frequent the canal and if you look closely at the water you may spot examples of these species. The footpaths are easy to follow and are fairly well-waymarked, although one or two stiles may cause some consternation as they are in poor condition.

Walk 2: Market Bosworth and the Ashby Canal

Distance: 7 miles

Maps: O.S. Landranger 140, Leicester and Coventry Area; O.S. Pathfinder 893 (SK20/30); O.S. Pathfinder 894 (SK40/50)

Location: Market Bosworth is bordered by the A447, A444 and B585 roads, some nine miles north of Hinckley or 10½ miles north of Nuneaton. The starting point for this walk is Bosworth Park, a country park, on Leicester Road. Grid reference 411030.

Parking: Car Park at Bosworth Park – Honesty Box, 50p

Refreshments: The Olde Black Horse (Good Food) – Market Bosworth. The Hercules Inn, Sutton Cheney. Bosworth Buttery Cafeteria – Bosworth Battlefield and Market Bosworth Tea Rooms.

Public Transport:

By Rail: Nearest British Rail station is at Hinckley

By Bus: Leicester/Market Bosworth and Hinckley/Market Bosworth services operated by Midland Fox or Stevensons

This walk follows the tow path of the Ashby canal between Sutton Cheney Wharf and Market Bosworth. Arguably it is the most scenic section of the canal. Step back into history and enjoy the sights and sounds of yester-year as you journey over the historic site of Bosworth Battlefield, pass alongside the Battlefield Steam Railway line, and tread the canal tow path where colourful narrowboats ply up and down at a leisurely pace. There are superb views of Shenton village from the aqueduct and picnic tables can be found in two places providing the walker with a comfortable stop.

The Route

It is a good idea to take some bread in your pocket in case the ducks decide to mug you as you walk over the grass in the park to the lake.

There are many horse chestnut trees in the park and during early autumn many fathers and sons are busy collecting conkers. A gravelled path leads into the arboretum and the easiest solution is to follow the path round to the left of this attractive wood to eventually reach a gate in the fence on the right. In spring the wood is a blaze of yellow with daffodils, primroses, celandine and many other wild plants. From the gate a grassy track leads to a tree-lined path and from here keen eyed walkers will see the Battlefield Flag to the right. Just past Looking Glass Pond are two stiles either end of a small wood. After crossing a track at Woodhouse Farm, follow a field perimeter path alongside Spinney Wood to a stream at the Duckery. Keep a hedge to the right and at a footpath junction bear right along the field perimeter path to a marker post. The views are typical South West Leicestershire with wide open aspects and arable fields on both sides of the footpath. Turn left, then bear diagonally right to the next marker post on to a very obvious field path with Sutton Cheney church ahead. At a lane join a grassy track to the right and if the strong smell of coffee at the Arms House restaurant fails to lure you in, continue ahead to the road and turn left.

Sutton Cheney is a picturesque village with an abundance of thatched cottages and a renown pub with oak beams called The Hercules Inn. Connoisseurs of good food and beer are recommended to call here as the pub's reputation is second to none. At the road junction turn right and walk along the road towards Dadlington for ½ mile to Sutton Cheney Wharf. This makes an ideal spot for a picnic and during the summer months picnic tables will be available for use by walkers. Do not cross over the canal bridge to the recognised tow path but walk along the footpath to a stile. Now a very pleasant woodland path passes through Ambion Wood to the entrance to the Battlefield.

It is but a short walk to the Battlefield Visitors Centre and time must be allowed to absorb the historic content of Leicestershire's most famous battle area. Join the battle trail and a signpost for Shenton station and King Richard's field points the way. Along the trail are information boards strategically placed identifying important parts of Bosworth Field where the battle raged. The church spire of Market Bosworth protrudes into the skyline and the undulating countryside stretches ahead for miles making this a strong vantage point.

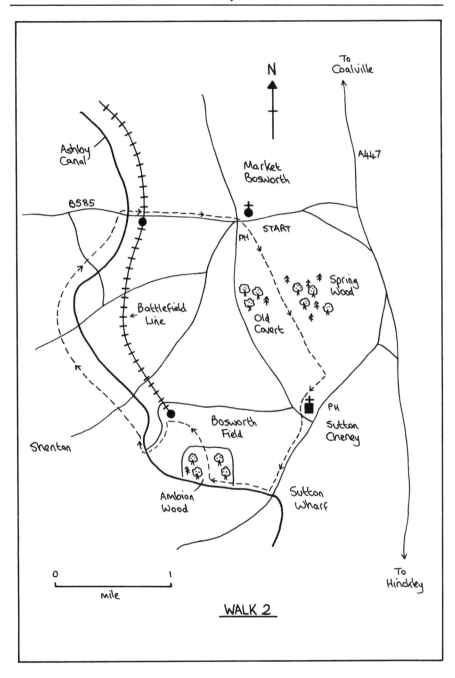

WALK 2

At Shenton station cross over the Battlefield line and pass through the car park to the road. Turn left along the road to the canal bridge and join the tow path over the bridge to the right. Shortly you will cross Shenton aqueduct, (there are only two aqueducts on the Ashby canal), and below the aqueduct are superb views of Shenton village. As you follow the tow path for the next two miles, a different sight awaits you around each corner as you pass beneath Wellsboro, Fox, Deakin's, Coton, and Jackson's bridges. All too soon Bosworth wharf bridge is reached and the canal walking section is completed.

Turn right on to the B585 crossing over the canal bridge, then the Battlefield line. Below is Market Bosworth station, the only intermediary stop on the preserved steam line. Follow the road ahead for one mile to reach Market Bosworth market place. Turn right, walk past the memorial to Rectory Lane, then turn left. A further 200 yards along Rectory Lane is the starting point of the walk at Bosworth Park.

Points of Interest

Market Bosworth is an attractive market town with many fine Georgian buildings centred around the market place. A Wednesday market has been in existence since 1285 and in recent years has become famous for its flower displays which got to the final of Britain in Bloom in 1988. Bosworth Country Park is an area of outstanding beauty with an arboretum, fishing lake, and children's play area.

Sutton Cheney church has a large squat tower and contains a plaque commemorating the memory of King Richard III who died at nearby Bosworth Field, having spent his last night near Sutton Cheney with 15,000 troops. The Hercules Inn serves wonderful food and is highly recommended.

Battle of Bosworth Field played host to armies from Richard III and Henry Tudor on 22nd August 1485 and the battle that ensued was Richard III's last stand in the War of the Roses. After this fateful encounter for Richard III, Henry Tudor was crowned Henry VII and ascended to the throne of England, thus ending 30 years of feuding between the great houses of York and Lancaster. There is a Battlefield Visitors Centre open from April to October each year, self guided battle trail that this walk partially follows and excellent refreshments at the Bosworth Buttery cafeteria.

The 14.30 to Market Bosworth at Shenton station

The Battlefield Line Steam Railway is located 400 yards from the Battlefield Visitors Centre at Shenton station. The line extends to Market Bosworth and Shackerstone, a distance of five miles. Owned by the Shackerstone Railway Society, the light railway operates steam trains on Sundays and Bank Holiday Mondays from April to October.

Shenton Aqueduct spans the road from Shenton to Far Coton and is approximately 30 feet long. As you cross the aqueduct, there are good views of the Battlefield and Shackerstone Railway along with the village below.

Footnote

The footpaths and tracks are very easy to follow with marker posts or waymark arrows in profusion. However, after heavy rain the tracks through continual walking by local ramblers will be very muddy and pot-holes of water can form. Ensure that stout walking boots are worn even if only part of the walk is to be undertaken. The footpath from Market Bosworth to Sutton Cheney and woodland path through Ambion Wood will be the worse for squelchy mud after wet weather.

Walk 3: Shackerstone and the Ashby Canal

Distance: 6½ miles

Maps: O.S. Landranger 140, Leicester and Coventry area; O.S. Pathfinder 893 (SK20/30)

Location: Shackerstone is sandwiched between the A444 and A447 roads, eight miles south of Measham or 10 miles north of Hinckley. The walk starts from the Rising Sun public house opposite the church. Grid reference 375067.

Parking: On the road outside the Rising Sun or inside the pub car park. (ask permission).

Refreshments: Rising Sun, Shackerstone. The Horse and Jockey, Congerstone. The Victoria Tea Rooms, Shackerstone Station. (Open daily except Mondays).

Public Transport:

By Rail: Nearest British Rail station is at Hinckley

By Bus: Nuneaton/Shackerstone Saturday only service operated by Bailliss Brothers.

Take a walk on the quiet side and visit three enchanting small villages of Shackerstone, Carlton, and Barton in the Beans in an unspoilt area tucked away in West Leicestershire. For connoisseurs of light railways then the headquarters of the Battlefield Line at Shackerstone Station must be inspected with the Victoria Tea Rooms at the station having hot food available throughout the day. Arguably the tow path that accompanies the Ashby Canal from Shackerstone to Carlton is probably the most picturesque part of the entire canal.

The Route

Opposite the church is the Rising Sun and Tudor Bar Grill Restaurant, the only pub in Shackerstone. It has a pleasant beer garden with a children's play area. The restaurant was previously a skittles alley and prior to that a cow shed. Keep the pub to your right and follow the road to a junction and turn right to reach the Ashby canal in about 100 yards, where an Ashby canal signpost indicates that Congerstone is 1½ miles to the right.

A narrowboat chugs along the Ashby Canal between Congerstone and Shackerstone

Join the tow path, then pass beneath bridge 52 and follow the canal away from Shackerstone sweeping round to the left. At Shackerstone moorings horse chestnut trees line the opposite bank and with sailing craft berthed beneath the trees it is a very desirable part of the canal tow-path. Go over the aqueduct bridging the River Sence and to the left Shackerstone Station and Battlefield line will be noted. There is a splendid view out to the right of Shackerstone church which is set in typical West Leicestershire pastoral countryside. Go beneath bridge 51 where there is a further Ashby canal signpost advising that Congerstone is now one mile away. The tow path meanders to bridge 50 then straightens out before bridge 49. On the right is Congerstone village and between bridge numbers 48 and 47 there are good views of the farming village. At bridge 47, a detour could be made to the Horse and Jockey public house just a mere 100 yards along the road that has a saddlery restaurant, à la carte menu, and bar meals available for the discerning walker.

The canal now curves away to the left and along this section of canal are Hinckley and Bosworth Borough Council seats for use by weary travellers. Between Bridges 46 and 45 the Ashby Canal is probably at its widest and in a further ½ mile leave the canal at Carlton bridge 44 and turn left to join the road. At the road junction turn left towards Twycross and follow this road for ½ mile to reach a public footpath signpost on the right.

Cross the short field to a stile, then walk over the track of the Battlefield Line ensuring that no train is powering towards you, to a stile. Follow the obvious field path, then keep a hedge close to your right that leads to a farm track. For the next ½ mile continue along the track ignoring the public footpath sign on the right. At the farm buildings, turn right and follow another track to the road and the outskirts of Carlton village. Turn left and walk into the village passing Old School Cottage to reach the Parish Church of St Andrew.

Opposite the church is a stile and public footpath sign where a narrow alleyway leads to a field stile. The path crosses a number of fields and is well-waymarked with numerous stiles spread out in the distance ahead with Barton in the Beans village seen slightly to the right. Eventually a farm track will be reached and this should be followed to the farm passing to the right of the farmhouse to emerge out onto a road in the village.

Turn left and walk through the pretty village of Barton in the Beans to reach a public bridleway sign on a corner at the end of the village. A track, which is rough to begin with, is followed from here and soon narrows into a grassy path. This is a popular bridleway and the local farmer has maintained it well by erecting a wire fence at the edge of his field thus enabling the good path to be created between the hedge and the fence. Go through a gate and bear right onto a footpath walking in the same direction. Pass a hand-carved wooden sign for Abbots Wood, then go through a gate before skirting a wood to the right to reach a farm track. Follow the track for ¼ mile, then pass beneath the Battlefield Line near to Shackerstone Station and cross the River Sence bridge. Go over the Ashby canal bridge back into Shackerstone and turn left where the Rising Sun is 100 yards on your left.

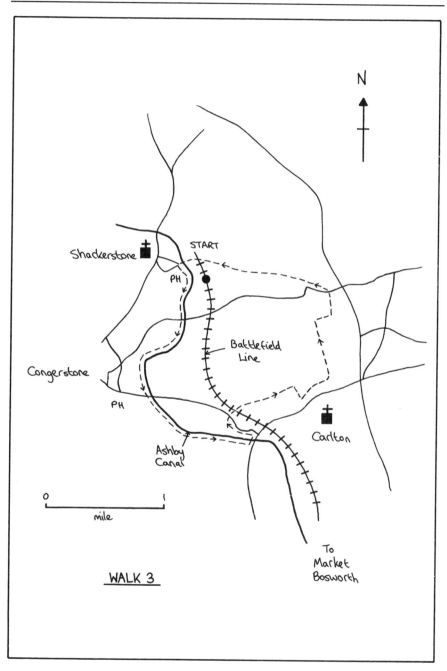

N

Shackerstone

START

PH

Battlefield
Line

Congerstone

PH

Carlton

Ashby
Canal

0 _____ 1
mile

WALK 3

To
Market
Bosworth

Points of Interest

Shackerstone is a most attractive village but has few amenities. It dates back to Saxon times and St Peter's Church stands proud in the centre of the village and is well worth visiting. Shackerstone is the base for The Battlefield Line, a preserved steam railway solely operated by volunteers, that runs to Shenton where access is available to the historic battlefield. The Shackerstone Railway Society celebrated their Silver Jubilee in 1994 and services operate at weekends between March and October with special 'Santa' services throughout December. The station was built in 1873 and has been lovingly restored by members of the preservation Society. A museum has many items from the last century with special emphasis being placed on local railway history. The Victoria Station Tea Rooms open daily, except for Mondays, where morning coffee, lunches and afternoon teas are available during the day.

Carlton is a small but very beautiful village with 'roses round the door' cottages and a classical style church built in 1764. The parish church of St Andrew is all brick being rebuilt in the late nineteenth century. The Victorian building is somewhat out of place in this quiet village.

Barton in the Beans is another small village with houses scattered along the road. Isolated in the winter, there is no pub or shop, but very desirable in the summer; the village name is synonymous with broad beans that have been grown in the area since medieval times.

Footnote

Allocate a day for this walk as there is plenty to see and enjoy in the area. The Ashby Canal is very pretty to follow with good views of rural countryside, all footpaths and bridleways are well-walked and signposted. Afterwards, spend some time poking about at Shackerstone Station and museum and perhaps even take in a trip to Shenton and back if time allows on the light steam railway.

Walk 4: Snarestone and the Ashby Canal

Distance: 6½ miles

Maps: O.S. Landranger 140, Leicester and Coventry area; O.S. Pathfinder 893 (SK20/30)

Location: Snarestone is located just off the B4116 road, three miles south of Measham and straddles the Ashby canal. The walk begins at the Globe Inn car park in the village. Grid reference 344094.

Parking: The Globe Inn, Snarestone (kind permission of the landlord)

Refreshments: The Globe Inn, Snarestone and The Belper Arms, Newton Burgoland.

Public Transport:

    By Rail: Nearest British Rail station is at Hinckley

    By Bus: Heather/Ashby de la Zouch service operated by Paul James coaches and Tamworth/Coalville service operated by Stevensons.

Beginning at the most northerly point of the Ashby canal at Snarestone, this vintage walk is steeped in tradition and history with the canal passing beneath the village and extending for a further half mile to its present day terminus. At Newton Burgoland is Leicestershire's oldest public house, The Belper Arms named after the Belper family. A wide choice of delightful home cooked bar meals are available but look out for 'Fred' the friendly resident ghost, who apparently has a liking for the ladies!

The Route

There can be no better starting point for a walk than from a pub and The Globe Inn at Snarestone is no exception. The children's play area is of the highest quality and the beer garden is most pleasant where a convivial drink can be enjoyed after the walk.

Go to the right of the pub car park, where a path leads down to

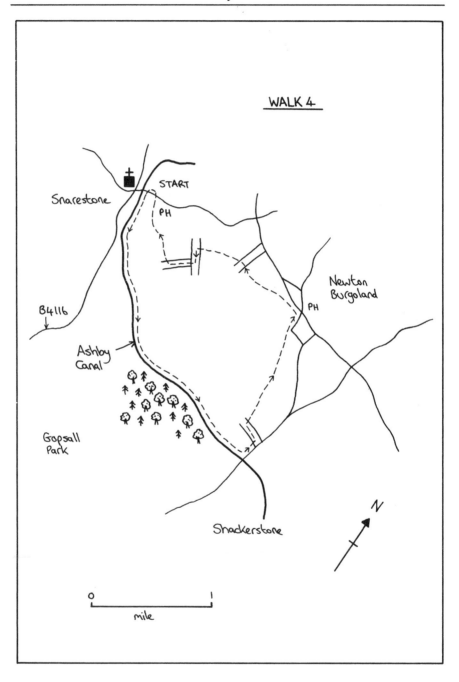

WALK 4

Snarestone

START

PH

Newton
Burgoland

PH

B4116

Ashby
Canal

Gopsall
Park

Shackerstone

N

0   1
mile

the tow path of the Ashby canal and immediately to the right is the entrance to Snarestone tunnel. Walk away from the tunnel entrance along the secluded grassy tow path and this section of the canal is very popular with anglers, during the fishing season, with angling matches often take place most weekends. Pass beneath bridge 59 and continue along the tow path reinforced with stones sunk into the ground which give additional support to walkers especially in times of wet weather. The canal here is very tranquil with great reed mace, yellow water lily, and marsh marigold all noted in flower along both banks in summer.

After bridge 58 is Gopsall Wharf where a picnic site has been created on the site of the old coal wharf. As late as the early 1980s boats were still being loaded with coal by lorries at the concrete landing apron and the apron is there today providing a secure angling platform for wheelchair users. The environment of the canal takes on a different perspective after bridge 57 as the tow path cuts through Reservoir Covert for ½ mile with trees overhanging the canal on both sides as far as Timms Bridge. From here onwards the tow path skirts to the left of Shackerstone Park, a large wood incorporating a number of small coverts. Look out for different kinds of dragon flies and damsel flies such as *Anex Imperator* and *Erythroma Najas* hovering above the vegetation by the canal side in the warmer months of the year. Continue along the canal tow path passing beneath bridge 54 and in a further ¾ mile leave the canal at bridge 53 near to the village of Shackerstone.

Walk along the road to the left for 200 yards, then turn left at a sign for Shackerstone Station to join a surfaced farm road. Continue along this farm road for ¼ mile to reach a public footpath sign on the right. An obvious field path well-waymarked leads to Fields Farm where a track is then joined. Continue along the track for ½ mile to eventually reach a gate and emerge out onto a road. Walk along the road into the unusually named village of Newton Burgoland to a road junction and turn left. The road leads past The Belper Arms, reputed to be the oldest public house in Leicestershire, to a footpath sign on the left. At the bottom of Nethercote turn left to Corner Farm where a public footpath sign will be found on the right.

Pass through the metal gate where a well-used footpath leads to a stream. Follow the field perimeter path to the right over Swepstone fields to reach a stile and a farm track. Climb the stile opposite then cross a short field to a hedge and marker post. Turn left keeping a hedge close to your right and from here the path is easy to follow. A stile on the right needs to be climbed then with the hedge to your left continue ahead to a farm road. Turn left, then in 100 yards turn right onto a track that is unsuitable for motors and skirt alongside a wood to the right to a public footpath sign on the right.

Keeping a hedge close to your left once again walk ahead on the field perimeter path to a hedge gap. Continue ahead now following a line of stiles to eventually reach a track that leads to the road. Turn left and walk back through Snarestone village passing the endowed school on the right to The Globe Inn.

Points of Interest

Snarestone Village is small and pleasant with the parish church of St Bartholomew dating back to 1732. This north west Leicestershire village straddles the Ashby canal by way of the 250 yard Snarestone tunnel and the Globe Inn is situated adjacent to the entrance of the tunnel. About ½ mile north of Snarestone is the current end of the canal and a beautiful Victorian building that was formerly the Hinckley Urban District Council pumping station. Built in 1892 the Victorian gothic waterworks supplied water to Hinckley but is no longer in use and has passed into private ownership.

Gopsall was a village with its own church and a magnificent Georgian House. The village has long since disappeared and the Hall was pulled down in 1951. It is reputed that Handel composed part of the "Messiah" while staying at Gopsall Hall as the guest of his friend Charles Jennens who had the Hall built after purchasing the estate in 1685. The park today is a mere shadow of its former self; the grounds are private and not open to the public.

Newton Burgoland is in the Parish of Swepstone with the village and St Peter Church one mile north. A small but slowly expanding village it takes its names from the Birgilon family which means Burgundian from medieval times. Not may public houses can boast having a resident friendly ghost but The Belper Arms in the village is home to "Fred". The ghost is famous for pinching ladies' bottoms but he hates men and is said to be searching to find his lost love. The pub itself is circa 1290 and was built originally to house the workers that built Swepstone church. Reputed to be the oldest pub in Leicestershire, for many years it was named the Shepherd and Shepherdess until Lord Belper bought the village and changed its name to The Belper Arms. Both the food and drink are recommended and there is an excellent beer garden at the rear.

Look out for 'Fred' the resident ghost at the Belper Arms

Footnote

An optional extra is to follow the tow path from Snarestone northwards to the conclusion of the canal just ½ mile away after completing the walk. The footpath from Newton Burgoland to Snarestone appears not to be walked too often and in places may be difficult to follow but provided you keep to the field perimeter hedge you will not go wrong.

Walk 5: Husbands Bosworth and The Grand Union Canal

Distance: 7½ miles

Maps: O.S. Landranger 140, Leicester and Coventry; O.S. Landranger 141, Kettering, Corby and surrounding area; O.S. Pathfinder 937 (SP68/78)

Location: Husbands Bosworth is a large village either side of the A427 road, about six miles west of Market Harborough. The walk starts from All Saints Church on Church Street at the junction with the A427 road. Grid reference 645845.

Parking: Roadside along Church Street – no official car park.

Refreshments: The Bell Inn, Husbands Bosworth – The Wharf Inn, Welford.

Public Transport:

By Rail: Nearest British Rail station is at Market Harborough

By Bus: Northampton/Leicester service calls at Husbands Bosworth and is operated by United Counties Omnibus Co. Ltd.

This walk is just the tonic to blow away any blues and stimulate the mind. It is also an ideal way to explore the pastoral scenery that is so characteristic of the area, close to the Northamptonshire border. The Welford Arm of the Grand Union Canal was completed in 1814 with one lock on its 1½ miles length. The walk from Welford marina to the junction is arguably the most attractive and tranquil in the county, while the path that goes through Husbands Bosworth tunnel is so unexpectedly steep that you may have to pause to draw breath before reaching the top.

The Route

With the church to your right, walk along High Street for 50 yards to a left turning into Butt Lane and continue to the end where a double bridleway sign will be located. Keep to the lane where in 100 yards it gives way to a farm track and offers many pleasant views of

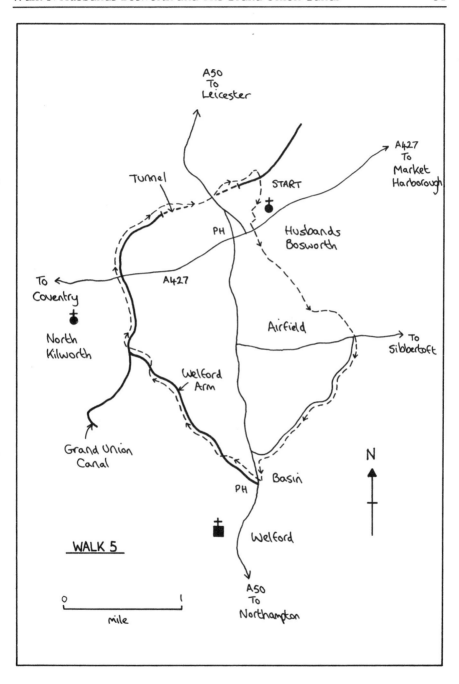

open pastoral countryside. The track is prone to collecting puddles of water after heavy rain but is not muddy.

Go through the double gates that allow vehicles to pass into the nearby sand and gravel extraction works, or if closed the adjacent gate, and continue to a metal gate. From here a grassy field path is taken and climbs slowly through rich green meadows while over to the left is a stream that forms the border between Leicestershire and Northamptonshire. In due course a bridle-gate is reached and access to the former wartime Husbands Bosworth airfield. In the 1960s the aerodrome was sold off and is now used by an assortment of businesses including the Coventry Flying Club. Care needs to exercised in the next section of the walk as the flying club use part of the old airfield for gliding purposes. Gliding takes place all week round and providing you follow the bridleway signs erected by the flying club and take heed of the notices, the airfield will be crossed without any trouble.

Turn left along the concrete track, then bear to the right to reach a public bridleway sign in about ¼ mile. Go through the metal gate and turn left onto a disused concrete runway alongside the landing and take off area looking out for any trailing tow ropes or cables. At the end of the disused runway is a public bridleway sign and notice that points the way across the actual runway strip. This is partially a permissive path given by the gliding club and should be crossed as quickly as possible when clear to the road bearing in mind that the path could be closed at any time by the flying club. It appears that at the end of the Second World War the course of the road was moved but the powers at Whitehall omitted to alter the right of way.

At the road junction opposite turn left to Welford 1½ miles and follow the road still passing through land of the former airfield noting to your right the shell of an old RAF building. A little further along the road is the new police building, where the police helicopter is housed, and is shared by both Leicestershire and Northamptonshire police forces. The helicopter gives vital air support and it is reputed that when airborne the helicopter's running costs are in the region of £7,000 per hour. Continue along the road for ¾ mile to pass the compact Welford Reservoir and a further ¼ mile brings you to the A50 road junction.

Turn left down the hill into Welford village as far as the Wharf Inn and the Grand Union Canal basin. Time should be spent at the

Wharf Inn where there is a canal garden and inside the pub are many old photographs depicting the former glory days of the Welford Arm of the Grand Union Canal. The "Arm" was completed in 1814 and was a terminus for the distribution of coal to the surrounding villages. Nearby are the reservoirs of Sulby, Welford and Naseby where water feeds into the basin of the canal ensuring that the water levels are kept constant along the canal. In 1969 the "Arm" was reopened to navigation with the marina being built in 1971. The present owner has tried to bring back commercial traffic to the canal arm by having deliveries of coal twice per year to the basin for his own personal use.

A narrowboat approaches Welford on the Welford Arm of the Grand Union Canal

Walk along the tow path to the right, soon leaving the marina behind; the area is very attractive, especially where the trees on either side of the canal meet and give an umbrella-like appearance. At Welford Lock, only three feet six inches deep, cross over the wooden footbridge and continue ahead on the grassy tow path now on the opposite bank. After a further ½ mile of gently meandering ignore the next wooden footbridge to a farm and in due course climb a stile alongside a gate. From here the canal begins to open out and at the next stone arch bridge pass through a gate and cross back again to the opposite bank at Bosworth Mill Farm. To the left the Leicester line of the Grand Union Canal is seen, and soon the canal junction is reached. Pass the sign post to reach bridge 42 and cross over to a stile and join the tow path.

Walk ahead passing beneath bridge 42 where there are superb views of rural countryside to the left with the church spire of North Kilworth seen protruding into the skyline. After passing beneath bridge 43 the moorings and marina at North Kilworth are reached. Here the A427 crosses the canal at bridge 45 and for the next mile the trees overhang the tow path as the canal dramatically bends round to the right to the entrance to Husband Bosworth tunnel in a deep cutting. The tunnel is 1166 yards in length and was opened in 1813 with the eastern portal being rebuilt in 1924.

From the tunnel entrance a flight of steps leads to the tow path that takes you onto the top of the tunnel and a gravelled track. The path over the tunnel is maintained by British Waterways and strictly speaking is a permissive path, not a right of way. The path climbs quite steeply before descending to the A50 road on the outskirts of the village. Go through a gate, cross the road and continue along the track to the old three arch railway bridge that took the Rugby-Peterborough railway line directly over the tunnel. The railway line was closed in 1966 but the old track bed is very visible.

A narrow woodland path runs adjacent to the railway cutting before rejoining the canal by the tunnel entrance. Ignore a set of steps on your right and in a short distance pass beneath bridge 46 (Honeypot Farm Bridge) where the canal is then left. Turn left along a track, take the second left along Church Lane, then bear right to reach the church in about 100 yards.

Points of Interest

Husbands Bosworth has a population of just under 1000 and is a large village close to Market Harborough. The village sits on a ridge between the Welland and Avon Valleys close to the Northamptonshire border. There are many interesting and attractive buildings and a little time should be spent in walking around the village. The church has a gilded slate clock face and a spire built in the fourteenth century. If in need of refreshments try the Bell Inn at the western end of the village.

Welford lies across the border in Northamptonshire and is a spacious village built mainly of brick. Welford's finest building is the church that over looks the Avon Valley. It contains a thirteenth-century font while the screens are Jacobean and the church itself is of varying dates. Two miles to the east of Welford is the site of the Battle of Naseby which history will recall was the last battle of the Civil War.

North Kilworth is a compact village of over 500 inhabitants and is part of a pair of villages close to the peaceful Avon Valley. The twelfth-century church is dedicated to St Andrew and is noted for its Jacobean "Armada" pulpit of Spanish oak. The old wharf has been converted into a thriving marina for narrowboats and is a useful supply centre for canal users.

Footnote

This is a splendid walk that all the family will enjoy. However, I must emphasise that the section through the gliding area must be treated with respect and care as the Coventry Flying Club have gone out of their way to accommodate walkers and expect that you will take a responsible attitude at all times on their land.

Walk 6: Laughton and the Grand Union Canal

Distance: 5½ miles

Maps: O.S. Landranger 141, Corby and surrounding area; O.S. Pathfinder 916 (SP69/79); O.S. Pathfinder 937 (SP68/78)

Location: Laughton is five miles west of Market Harborough and the best way to approach the village is from the A427 road. At Lubenham village take the turn to Foxton Locks, then turn left immediately until reaching a sign for Laughton on the right. The walk starts at the telephone box opposite the village green. Grid reference 659889.

Parking: With difficulty around The Green

Refreshments: No refreshments available. However, a short detour to Gumley village will reward you with refreshments at the Bell Inn.

Public Transport:

    By Rail: Nearest British Rail station is at Market Harborough

    By Bus: No bus service to Laughton.

Take a fascinating stroll over the top of the Laughton Hills on well-used footpaths and bridleways experiencing many spacious views of dogmatic rural south-west Leicestershire countryside. The Grand Union Canal meanders at the foot of the wooded slopes of the hills and this stretch of waterway is extremely attractive to follow especially between Lubenham Lodge and Theddingworth Lodge. After leaving the canal at bridge 52 be prepared for a steep climb through the hills back to Laughton.

The Route

Laughton is a small village with a myriad of footpaths radiating from many different points and care needs to be exercised at the start of the walk to ensure that the correct footpath is taken.

Stand with your back to the telephone box, looking at the village

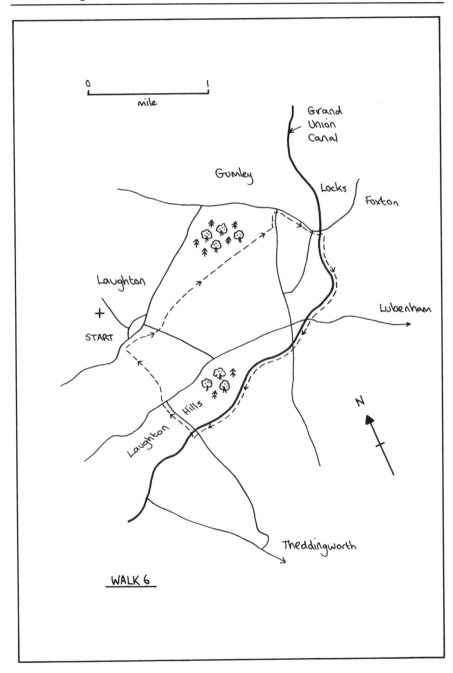

0 _____ 1
mile

Grand
Union
Canal

Gumley

Locks

Foxton

Laughton

Lubenham

+

START

Laughton Hills

Laughton

N

Theddingworth

WALK 6

green, and turn right onto the Theddingworth Road where in 100 yards a public footpath sign will be located on the right. Pass through two farm gates then bear left over a stile, and cross a series of short fields and stiles to a double stile that leads you out onto the road. A public footpath sign opposite points the way across the next field and from the hilltop there is a wonderful view of the rolling countryside ahead, especially of Gumley Covert seen to the left.

After crossing a double stile an arable field footpath is joined that acts as a tread between the higher and lower part of the field. Continue ahead ensuring that a hedge is kept to your right to an open gateway, then turn through a gate on the right. Keeping the hedge now to the left continue ahead to a large gap in the hedge adjacent to a farmers track that veers off to the right. Go over an unkempt field to a waymark post, then cross a stream and follow this stream to the field corner and gate by a road. Turn left along the road for 200 yards to a public bridleway sign, and pass through a wooden gate into a field. Cross a short field to a road and here a choice has to be made whether to take a short diversion to the village of Gumley, to the left, for refreshments at the Bell Inn or to turn right and continue with the walk. Whatever you decide, the walk continues from this point along a section of quiet road walking for about ½ mile, mainly uphill, and this brings you to the Grand Union Canal above the famous staircase of locks at Foxton.

Cross over the road bridge to join the tow path on the left-hand side of the canal and walk away to the left from Foxton Locks and bridge 60. The tow path is very uneven and narrow in places, especially when crossing the overspill weir but by the time bridge 59 is reached the path returns to a more orthodox and grassy surface. There are many good views of the countryside between bridge 59 and bridge 58 and just before reaching the latter bridge is Lubenham Lodge, a fine old building with mature trees all around set beneath the Laughton Hills.

In quick succession pass beneath two fine brick arch bridges numbers 57 and 56, ignoring the stile and footpath at bridge 56 that goes to Marston Trussell. This section of tow-path is very pretty with the hills forming a superb backcloth and after passing beneath bridge 55 a GJC Company sign post will be seen stating that Leicester is 20 miles. At bridge 54 the village of Theddingworth nestles below in the Welland Valley while at bridge 53 the canal narrows to pass beneath the farm bridge. All too quickly bridge 52 is reached and it is time to leave the canal and head into the Laughton Hills by joining the narrow road from Laughton to Theddingworth. Turn right over the bridge and follow the steep road not forgetting to look back for a panoramic view of the Welland Valley before reaching the Mowsley-Foxton road. Cross to a gated road to Laughton opposite and pass through Laughton Lodge Farm gate where a surface track leads you around the farm buildings to the right to a farm gate.

A bridle track is now followed, and although a sign post indicated back at the road junction that this was a gated road it would be extremely hard for a car to pass along the track without getting into difficulty. A pleasant stroll of ½ mile along this green track through pretty open countryside eventually brings you to a farm gate which may be surrounded by mud and water. Go through the gate and to your right is the telephone box and opposite is the village green which signals the end of the sumptuous walk in this delightful part of the county.

A vintage car beneath the oak tree on Laughton's village green

Points of Interest

Laughton is one of the most elegant of villages to be found in Leicestershire perched on top of the miniature Laughton Hills. There are few facilities in the village but judging by the vast number of footpaths and bridleways in the locality it is a paradise for walkers and horse riders. St Luke's church, at the north end of the village, was built in the thirteenth century and has an interesting bell tower.

Lubenham Village has a population of over 1200, some two miles west of Market Harborough and is set in the Welland Valley. The Coach and Horses public house is worth driving to after the walk for refreshments as is the low squat church of All Saints with its Georgian pews and medieval wall paintings. Several large houses in the village were constructed in the late nineteenth century as hunting boxes.

Footnote

The discerning walker will not be disappointed with this circular route – it is a real gem. A plethora of magnificent scenic views await you from every footpath and this walk could be followed time and time again without losing its freshness. Regretfully, there is no public house to call at for refreshments but an open air picnic in such beautiful surroundings is just as agreeable.

Walk 7: Market Harborough and The Grand Union Canal

Distance: 9 miles

Maps: O.S. Landranger 141, Kettering, Corby and surrounding area; O.S. Pathfinder 937 (SP68/78)

Location: Market Harborough is 15 miles south of Leicester strategically placed at the junction of the A6 and A427 roads. The walks starts from the Market Harborough arm canal basin at the rear of the Six Packs Inn on the A6 road. Grid reference 726878.

Parking: At the canal basin by the Six Packs Inn.

Refreshments: Six Packs Inn, Market Harborough. The Black Horse, Foxton (recommended)

Public Transport:

By Rail: Nearest British Rail station is at Market Harborough

By Bus: Leicester/Market Harborough frequent service operated by Midland Fox.

The Market Harborough arm of the Grand Union Canal from Foxton Locks to Market Harborough is 5¾ miles. This walk from the basin to Foxton Village follows 5¼ miles of tranquil river like appearance canal. The Market Harborough basin is famous for hosting the first ever canal rally in Britain in 1950 and is today subject to an ambitious scheme of redevelopment, much needed in this area. Returning from the beautiful village of Foxton a series of well-way-marked paths makes this a walk to remember.

The Route

The canal basin is located behind the old canal pub, the Six Packs Inn of Leicestershire, which is named after the six fox hunting packs that hunt in the county. Go through a gap, if the entrance gate is locked, into the boatyard and follow the path towards the building of the Anglo-Welsh Narrowboats; Harborough Marine Limited and pass round to the left of this building and workshop to gain access to the tow path on the left of the canal.

Market Harborough Basin at the end of the Grand Union canal

Before setting off on the walk be sure to look back at the canal basin where many of the old wharf buildings still stand but are now becoming dilapidated and in need of repair. At the time of writing, a row of workers' cottages at the far end of the canal basin was noticeably unstable.

At the start of the tow path the ground is uneven and after heavy rain it is liable to wet and muddy. Many houses on the opposite bank have beautiful well-kept lawns that stretch down to the water's edge and squirrels may be seen playing on these lawns and climbing the over-hanging trees that gives a romantic feel to the canal. Quite soon the tow path becomes easy to walk along due to the resurfacing improvements carried out by British Waterways.

The canal drifts to the left and there are many fine views of Harborough District countryside to take in and after about one mile the first bridge is reached over the canal. Known locally as the

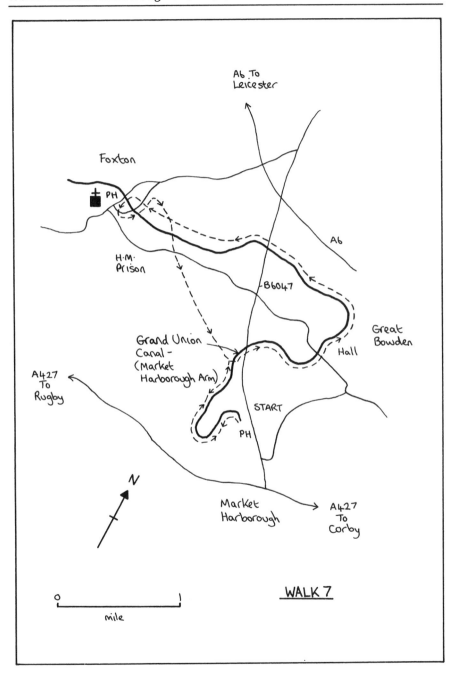

A6 To
Leicester

Foxton

PH

H·M·
Prison

A6

B6047

Great
Bowden

Grand Union
Canal –
(Market
Harborough Arm)

Hall

A427
To
Rugby

START

PH

N

Market
Harborough

A427
To
Corby

0   1
mile

WALK 7

wooden bridge, a footpath crosses the canal here from the A6 road to Foxton and we will be returning along this footpath later. In 50 yards the gravelled tow path takes on a more riverside like appearance and becomes very grassy.

At a stone bridge, cross over to the opposite bank and continue ahead to pass beneath bridge 12, Uncle Tom's Bridge, which takes the busy A6 road over the canal. An extremely pleasant grassy tow path leads you to bridge 11, Saunts Bridge, and in a short time bridge 10, Bowden Hall Bridge, is reached. By the road bridge over the canal is the sixteenth century, Great Bowden Hall, which is a most impressive sight to the casual observer. The canal and tow path once again bears to the left with further glorious views of undulating countryside and after passing beneath the next stone arch farm bridge the village of Thorpe Langton will be noted to the right.

A further mile of peaceful walking is brought to an abrupt halt by reaching Croda Colloids Ltd, where animal carcases are turned into adhesives and glue, by bridge 8, Gallows Hill Bridge. Follow the canal around to the left below Gallows Hill some 337 feet high where further extensive views to the right prevail. Pass beneath bridge 7, Johnson's Bridge, and between this bridge and the next bridge no 6, Sedgely's Bridge, you may be lucky enough to see one or a pair of herons that regularly frequent this part of the canal.

From Sedgely's Bridge, the village of Foxton is seen to the right, and in a short distance bridge 5, Clarkes Bridge, will be reached. Continue ahead to a unusual swing bridge in Foxton that is key operated by canal users to open and close. Pass by the start of Foxton moorings, then leave the canal at the next bridge by a Leicestershire Round Footpath sign and cross over the bridge to the Black Horse public house on Main Street where suitable refreshments may be enjoyed. The half whitewashed pub was rebuilt in 1900 on the site of an old coaching inn, and has a beer garden and patio together with a extensive range of beers and hot meals.

By the Parish Church of St Andrew, turn left and walk along Swingbridge Street passing through a most interesting part of Foxton Village to the Swingbridge. Just beyond Foxton Lodge is a bridleway and footpath sign on the right. At the end of the track is a stile and public footpath sign where a well-used field path crosses several short fields to reach the Grand Union canal again.

This time cross over Sedgley's Bridge to a join another well-used field footpath and follow up hill to a stile and the road. Cross to a waymark post opposite, where a path leads away from the road to the left to a stile. On the right is the imposing H.M. Prison, Gartree, that was originally a maximum security prison but has now been downgraded to a lower level secure unit. The path here is well-way-marked and needs little explanation until Larks model aeroplane flying club is reached. Pass to the left of the hut, and keeping a hedge close to your right, take care in walking through the clay pigeon shooting field to a home made signpost. Bear right towards the A6 to join a clear field grassy path to a waymark post. A short field perimeter path leads to a stile and access to the canal, by the wooden bridge. Re-join the tow path and walk to the right now retracing your earlier steps back to Market Harborough basin and the Six Packs Inn of Leicestershire on Leicester Road.

Points of Interest

Market Harborough has a population of 17,000 and is the largest town in Harborough District. The district itself is the largest within the county, covering some 230 square miles with 25 miles of the Grand Union Canal meandering through the peaceful countryside. As its name implies Market Harborough is a market town, and it is known that a market has existed since 1204. The town dates back to Medieval times and its names is a corruption of 'Haver Burgh' (oat hill). The town is dominated by the thirteenth century Parish Church of St Dionysus which has one of the finest spires in England soaring to 161 feet above High Street. Built of smooth grey limestone it is much in contrast to the church which is of ironstone.

Harborough Museum at the Council Offices on Adam and Eve Street is well worth a visit as the social history of Market Harborough and the surrounding area may be traced from Medieval times up to the present day. There is a local bootmakers' workshop and corsetry display to look over. The museum is open Monday-Saturday, 10.00 – 16.30 Sunday, 14.00 – 17.00, closed Good Friday and December 25th/26th.

Great Bowden is the original settlement of Market Harborough and within its parish in the twelfth century the new town of Market Harborough developed. The village retains its own identity and is noted for a series of greens surrounded by rows of houses and cottages. One green still retains the nineteenth-century granite horse trough erected by the Metropolitan Drinking Fountain and Cattle Trough Association for the welfare of horses.

Foxton is an ancient village dominated by the square tower of St Andrews Parish Church. The tower is thirteenth century standing on a hill at the top of the village and can be seen from many miles away. The Grand Union canal bisects the village and the hump back bridge was once the entrance to Foxton Wharf.

Footnote

A walk of this length necessitates the need to wear walking boots or stout shoes as at the beginning of the tow path it is likely to be muddy especially after heavy rain. Several of the fields that are crossed are arable and if ploughed are very demanding to walk over.

Walk 8: Foxton Locks and the Grand Union Canal

Distance: 5 miles

Maps: O.S. Landranger 141, Kettering, Corby and surrounding area; O.S. Pathfinder 937 (SP68/78); O.S. Pathfinder 916 (SP69/79)

Location: Foxton Locks are five miles north of Market Harborough and signposted from either A6 road or A427 road from Lubenham. The walk commences from Foxton Locks Country Park. Grid reference 692892.

Parking: Foxton Locks Country Park car park — 50p charge

Refreshments: Bridge 61 Pub at Foxton Locks Basin. The Bell Inn, Gumley.

Public Transport:

   By Rail: Nearest British Rail station is at Market Harborough

   By Bus: Market Harborough/Foxton/Leicester infrequent service operated by Midland Fox. Winforfar Travel also run an infrequent service from Market Harborough to Foxton.

Foxton Locks is a popular beauty spot with a well-patronised pub at the bottom lock. It is the ideal starting point for this interesting family walk. Stride back into history and visit a unique staircase of 10 locks rising through the heart of the Leicestershire Countryside. View the canal museum and inclined plane where between 1900-1910 a Victorian steam-powered boat lift was used to by-pass the 10 locks. It is now under restoration and the boiler house has been reconstructed as a museum by the Foxton Inclined Plane Trust which gives the full story of Foxton Locks and Grand Union Canal.

The Route

At the entrance to the car park is a signpost for Foxton Locks and canal and this is where the walk begins. A specially constructed path by Leicestershire County Council runs adjacent to Gumley road which should be followed to the Grand Union Canal and to a

A busy scene at Foxton Basin. To the left is the Market Harborough Arm and to the right are the Bridge 61 pub and the Leicester Line of the Grand Union Canal

footbridge. Cross canal bridge 60 and join the tow path to the right and follow for ¼ mile to Foxton Top Lock and lock keeper's cottages where there is a beautifully kept garden and historical exhibition of the locks.

Descend by the staircase of 10 locks to the basin below noting to the right the canal museum and remnants of the inclined plane. From the locks there are superb views of the Leicestershire country-side stretching ahead as far as the eye can see. Keep to the left of the basin passing "Vagabond" pleasure cruise office to bridge 62 noting the Market Harborough arm of the Grand Union Canal disappearing to the right.

Go over the bridge then turn left along the tow path and the canal here is extremely busy with narrow boats and cruisers passing in and out of Foxton Basin. The tow path is jealously guarded by a high hedge to the right but good views prevail to the left. A "Vagabond" cruise boat may pass you here and after going beneath bridge 64 the landscape changes dramatically with rolling hills forming a perfect backcloth. Keep a sharp eye out for different kinds of water birds and the ever changing scene provides a delight for the naturalist. At

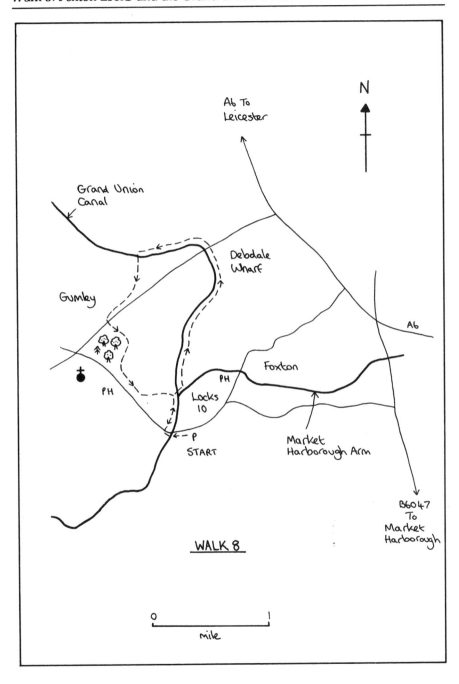

N

A6 To Leicester

Grand Union Canal

Debdale Wharf

Gumley

A6

Foxton

PH

PH

Locks 10

← P

START

Market Harborough Arm

B6047 To Market Harborough

WALK 8

0   1
mile

bridge 65 is Debdale Wharf and, to your left, rows of narrowboats will be seen in the boatyard awaiting engine repair or temporarily moored. The tow path sweeps round to the left and views of Smeeton Westerby and Kibworth Beauchamp villages are seen to the right. Continue along the tow path for a further ½ mile to bridge 68 which is a metal farm bridge and leave the canal by climbing the bank to a stile.

Join the footpath that crosses the bridge where a stile leads you to onto an obvious field path. Cross diagonally right to a gate where a track brings you out onto a road at Debdale Grange. In the distance the 10 locks of Foxton can be picked out just below the skyline. Turn right along the road for ¼ mile to a double footpath signpost and a stile, then head towards Gumley Woods to a marker post and skirt around the wood to the left to reach a stile. Cross to a hill opposite – if you are lucky a kestrel may be seen hovering overhead – and climb the hill, ignoring a path to your left, to reach a kissing gate in Gumley Village.

Turn left through the quaint village, where there is a distinct lack of lamp posts. Pass the Bell Inn to the right that serves morning coffee, light snacks, and evening meals. Then descend the hill towards Foxton to reach a public bridleway sign on the left. Pass through the gate and follow the obvious field path with a hedge to your left to eventually reach a gate. A track now leads to Foxton bottom lock and refreshments should be taken at the Bridge 61 pub. Ascend the staircase of 10 locks and retrace your steps to Foxton Locks Country Park car park.

Points of Interest

Foxton Locks were opened on 1st October 1812 and built as two staircase flights of five locks with side pounds set alongside and a passing point for boats midway. Each lock is only seven feet wide whereas the normal width of locks between Leicester and Foxton is 15 feet. The pound system works quite simply with the top gates of one lock becoming the bottom gates of the next lock; water passes from one lock into the side pound or pond and back into the next lock to equalise the levels. In all, water rises a full 75 feet and the staircase of locks are 300 yards long with the top lock 425 feet above sea level. Normally, it should take a boat no longer than one hour to complete the operation of passing through all the locks. At the bottom lock and basin the waterway interest is immense with Bridge 61 pub serving real ale and has a canal side garden. Foxton Boat Services Ltd run return pleasure cruises to Gumley Fields and also horse-drawn return canal trips to Foxton village, both taking 30 minutes.

Foxton Inclined Plane was an extraordinary Victorian steam-powered boat lift opened in 1900 to by-pass the staircase of locks with the aim of saving water and improving canal trade. The plane consisted of two counter-balancing water tanks resting on carriages that ran on rails which would take a 70 ton barge or two narrowboats up and down the hill. The locks were closed and for 10 years the Inclined Plane was a roaring success with journey times reduced to 12 minutes. However, mechanical problems, high running costs and competition from the railways brought about the downfall of this ingenious scheme and 1911 the Inclined Plane was closed to traffic and the locks reopened. The Plane remained in existence until 1928 when it was broken up and sold for scrap value.

Foxton Inclined Plane Trust was formed in 1980 with the sole purpose of restoring the old barge lift site and have made wonderful progress. To date the old boiler house has been reconstructed into the Canal Museum at the Middle Lock where the full story of the Inclined Plane is told with a trail over the site that must be followed. The museum is open every day in the summer, weekends and limited days in the winter.

Gumley is a small village of about 110 inhabitants who mainly live on either side of the road that passes through the village. St Helen's church was built in the grounds of Gumley Hall now unfortunately demolished but in its time was a building of grandeur.

Footnote

Do not be put off by the crowds of sightseers that flock to Foxton Locks if walking at a weekend, as they will be left behind in a matter of 300 yards from the bottom lock. This is a fine family walk with waterside interest for all ages and the tow path has been revamped in places making it easy to walk along, with the whole area supporting a large range of wildlife.

Walk 9: Smeeton Westerby and The Grand Union Canal

Distance: 5½ miles

Maps: O.S. Landranger 141, Kettering, Corby and surrounding area; O.S. Pathfinder 916 (SP69/79)

Location: Smeeton Westerby is 10 miles south east of Leicester and eight miles north of Market Harborough. Travel along the A6 road to Kibworth Beauchamp and follow signs for the village. The walk starts at the Kings Head public house, Main Street, near to the village hall. Grid reference 680929.

Parking: Roadside parking in village — no official car park.

Refreshments: The Kings Head, Smeeton Westerby. Queens Head, Saddington

Public Transport:

By Rail: Nearest British Rail station is at Leicester or Market Harborough.

By Bus: Market Harborough/Burton Overy service operated by Win-For-Far Travel. No Sunday service.

Blend together idyllic countryside with open stretches of canal and the result is a walk of sheer perfection. From the quiet and charming village of Smeeton Westerby well-used footpaths lead to the Grand Union Canal, which wriggles beneath the Smeeton Hills, that form a most exhilarating backcloth. Curiously this section of canal has no locks and there are different styles of bridges, some old and some new to reflect upon. The climax of the canal walk is Saddington Tunnel, which is walked over, and from above the tunnel entrance at each end are magnificent views to digest. A long but interesting track, full of surprises, returns you to the village for well-earned refreshments at the pub.

The entrance to Saddington Tunnel seen from the north, near to Fleckney

The Route

Walk along Main Street, with the Kings Head to your right passing the village hall to Debdale Lane and turn left. At the end of the lane a gate emits you onto a track where in 100 yards a public footpath sign is reached on the right. Climb the stile, and cross to the waymark post opposite keeping a small farm building to your right. Turn left onto a vague field path and it will soon be obvious where the next marker post is located at the far end of the field.

Go through two gates either side of a stream then follow the field perimeter path to the right ignoring a gate in the corner of the field. Cross a stile that is secluded in the hedge a little further round to your right and follow the obvious field path towards to a tree then to the left of the wooden telephone posts to a stile. If you look back there are glorious views of Smeeton Westerby village while in front of you Debdale Grange keeps a watchful eye over your progress from the top of Gumley Hill. A short field path now leads to a white metal footbridge over the Grand Union Canal.

Turn right onto the tow path and follow ahead passing beneath Gumley Road Bridge Number 69 after ½ mile. To the left there is a good view of Smeeton Hill, that stands over 500 feet, and the canal now twists and turns before reaching Long Hill Bridge, number 70. The villages of Smeeton Westerby and Kibworth Beauchamp are now close to your right and in due course the tow path veers sharply around to the left to pass beneath a typical farm stone bridge. A further 100 yards brings you to Smeeton Bends where the canal has been dredged and much improved by British Waterways. A feeder stream will be seen on the left that supplies water to the canal from Saddington Reservoir.

The next ½ mile finds the canal passing through some very ordinary countryside before reaching Smeeton Road Bridge, number 72, built in 1917. From here you may wish to make a detour to Saddington Village, about 1 mile to the west along the road, and perhaps enjoy refreshments at the Queens Head public house. Some 300 yards ahead is the entrance to Saddington Tunnel but unfortunately or fortunately depending on your sense of adventure there is no tow path through the underground passage. When boats first passed through the tunnel "leggers", men who lay on the boat and pushed along the tunnel walls with their legs, where needed until a steam tug was introduced.

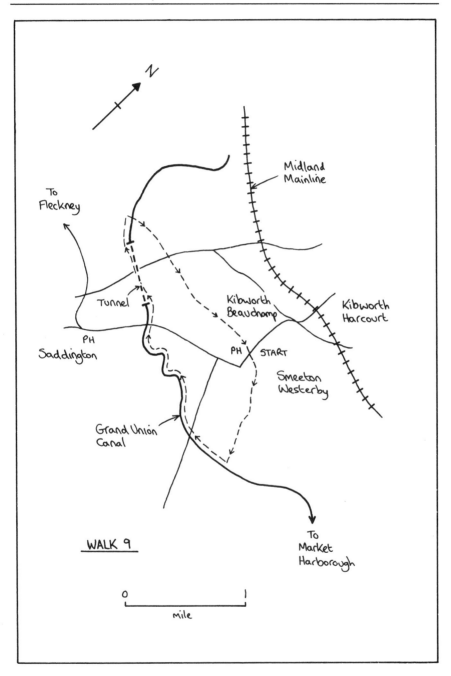

N

To
Fleckney

Midland
Mainline

Tunnel

Kibworth
Beauchamp

Kibworth
Harcourt

PH
Saddington

PH   START

Smeeton
Westerby

Grand Union
Canal

WALK 9

To
Market
Harborough

0 |

mile

A path leads away from the tunnel entrance and climbs above the canal onto a track that follows the line of the tunnel. Do remember to look back to experience the delightful view of the canal and surrounding hills. The well-used track eventually brings you to the Saddington Road and opposite a gate gives further access to the track above the tunnel. In due course a footpath junction is reached just before the tunnel end and the path that crosses from left to right is to be ignored. As you descend to the canal tow path on your left further views of the canal ahead are enjoyed. Continue along the tow path now for a further ½ mile to reach Fleckney Bridge, number 73, and after passing beneath the bridge leave the canal by turning left through a gate and cross over the bridge.

A well-waymarked field path is followed away from the canal and a footpath that runs off to the left must be ignored. Continue ahead to join a field track and pass to the right of an electricity sub station to a gate where a short field path leads to the Saddington Road once again. Cross to a gravelled lane opposite and very quickly turn sharp right, then left and from here onwards it is very easy to follow the lane to Smeeton Westerby. The lane extends for about 1¼ miles with periodically waymarkers placed along the way, although in reality there is no need for them.

As you near to the village there is a fine view of neighbouring Kibworth Beauchamp with the church standing dignified above the roof tops of the houses. Walk along Mill Lane and in due course the Kings Head pub will be reached on Main Street and the conclusion of a most satisfying walk.

Points of Interest

Smeeton Westerby is a small village about one mile south of Kibworth Beauchamp and is set in pretty undulating countryside. The little church of Christ Church was built in 1852 by Woodyer and has no tower but it is worth visiting as is the Kings Head pub for refreshments.

Saddington Tunnel is 880 yards long passing beneath hills that are over 450 feet high. The tunnel has an interesting history and none more so than when it was first built. It appears that work began in July 1795 and upon completion it was discovered that the tunnel had not been built straight which necessitated further expense and time in correcting the earlier mistakes. Eventually the tunnel was opened in early 1797 and today carries a preservation order as a population of bats have taken up residence inside the tunnel.

Kibworth Beauchamp and Kibworth Harcourt are known in general terms as 'Kibworth' but are two separate villages divided by the A6 road and Midland Main Line Railway. Kibworth takes its name from Saxon times and means "fort". A fort was built here, being part of a chain of forts knows to exist in this part of the county during those times. The Fernie Fox Hunt meets on occasion at Kibworth Beauchamp and the land around Smeeton Westerby is known to be a favourite of the hunt.

Footnote

This is a good family walk as there is plenty to see along the Grand Union Canal with the added bonus of watching narrowboats emerge into and out of Saddington Tunnel . Be sure to look through the dark underground passage as this will prove the old proverb that light does indeed exist at the end of the tunnel!

Walk 10: Kilby and the Grand Union Canal

Distance: 7 miles

Maps: O.S. Landranger 140, Leicester and Coventry area; O.S. Landranger 141, Kettering, Corby and surrounding area; O.S. Pathfinder 916 (SP69/79)

Location: Kilby is located seven miles south of Leicester just off the A50 Leicester-Northampton road. The walk begins from the Dog and Gun pub in the centre of the village. Grid reference 622954.

Parking: Dog and Gun pub car park (ask first) or on Main Street in village.

Refreshments: Dog and Gun, Kilby. The Old Crown, Fleckney.

Public Transport:

By Rail: Nearest British Rail station is at South Wigston

By Bus: Leicester/Kibworth frequent service operated by Midland Fox.

Hidden away in a quiet corner of South Leicestershire are the three villages of Kilby, Newton Harcourt and Fleckney. The Grand Union Canal passes close to these villages, all interesting in their own right, and runs through woods and beautiful parkland adjoining Wistow Park. From the canal tow path there is a magnificent view of the Norman Church at Wistow. This area is steeped in history and tradition with Charles I sheltering at Wistow Hall after his defeat at the Battle of Naseby in 1645.

The Route

Keeping the Dog and Gun public house on the right walk along Main Street to its junction with Wistow Road and follow round to the left. At the end of the village a public footpath sign and stile will be discovered, well hidden in the hedge, on the left that points to Newton Harcourt. Immediately cross a footbridge over a stream that is guarded at either end by a stile, and head for a marker post in the far corner of the field. Continue ahead over a number of grassy fields on the well-waymarked path to eventually reach a track.

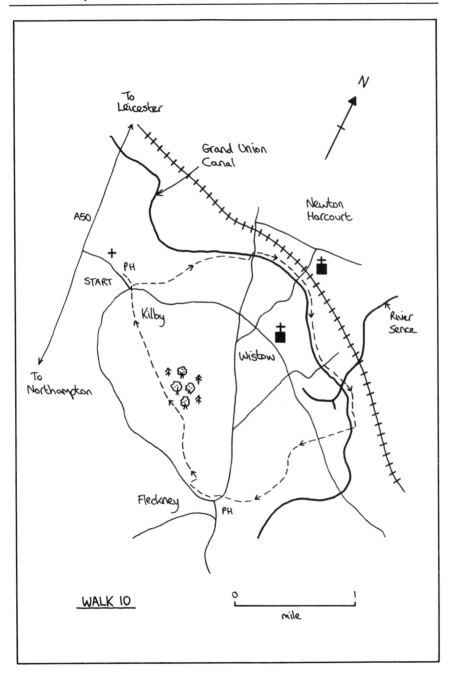

WALK 10

In due course the track widens out slightly and on either side are small paddocks, often with frisky horses. Keep your eyes peeled for unusual birds such as yellow buntings and goldfinches darting in and out of the mature hedge on the right. Just before the farm climb a stile on the left and walk around the rear of the building in the direction of the yellow waymark arrows. Join the path alongside the Grand Union Canal, pass quickly through a wood noting Top Half Mile Lock to the left. This is not the actual tow path but a footpath that runs adjacent to the canal which in due course reaches a road. Turn left over the canal road bridge and join the tow path to the left then pass beneath the road bridge.

The Lock-keeper's cottage and Top Lock at Newton Harcourt

After a short distance along the tow path, Spinney Lock will be passed and a further ¼ mile brings you to Newton Top Lock where an attractive lock keeper's cottage is encountered. The tow path is extremely pretty to walk along with rushes growing along the side of the canal and in places the water is quite shallow. Pass beneath bridge No 80 where, in summer, swallows may be seen swooping a few feet above the water level in search of insects. There is a dramatic curve to the right of the canal and, after passing beneath

High Bridge, number 79, there are excellent views of South Leicestershire. At the next bridge the fine church of Wistow, secluded in the trees, is seen and the Midland Main Line Railway is again on the left. Cross over the aqueduct of the River Sence, noting below major improvements carried out by British Waterways in the routing of the river, and at Cranes Lock the canal tow-path must be left.

Cross over Cranes Bridge where a footpath leads over two fields to a road. Opposite is a public footpath sign; the field perimeter path must be followed to the left to a waymark post where an arrow gives direction over the next field. The village of Fleckney is now seen ahead. After crossing a footbridge continue ahead on the obvious path noting Wistow Grange Farm to your left. A well-waymarked path crosses a number of fields to the village of Fleckney. At the road turn left, past the Conservative Club, to Kilby Road and walk along the road for a ¼ mile as far as Highfield Street. About 50 yards along this road on the left is a public footpath sign and an alleyway leads past the school playing fields. When reaching a housing estate, turn right then left to regain the footpath and alleyway.

Climb a stile into a paddock and, from here, one stile leads to another for the next ½ mile. The stiles become more spaced out but the field footpath is very easy to follow with marker posts and arrows pointing the way. Bear left over a stile and onto a path sandwiched between a sprouting hedge and metal fence and during the summer months of our climate the path is difficult to walk along as the grass underfoot becomes very long. If wearing shorts it is advisable to slip on a pair of over trousers to protect your legs. Skirt to the left of Fox Covert, then an obvious field path cuts away to the left to a stile. Cross a bridleway running from left to right, and although the village is less than an a mile away it is hidden out of sight.

It is now a question of crossing a number of small green fields perhaps avoiding the cows or sheep quietly going about their business for the next ¾ mile climbing stiles as and when they appear. Go through a brown gate, where the rooftops of the houses in Kilby village appear to lie on the ground like great pieces of corrugated cardboard, and a field track leads to a stile at the top of a farmyard. Go through the farmyard to emerge out onto Main Street, Kilby and the Dog and Gun is 100 yards away to your left.

Points of Interest

Kilby is a small prosperous village of about 300 inhabitants often referred to as "The Turnpike". One of the oldest buildings in Kilby is the Dog and Gun public house and part of the pub dates back to the seventeenth century although the other part is a mere 200 years old. The church of St Mary Magdalen was rebuilt in 1858 and stands well away from the village centre. In times of the Domesday Book the village was recorded as encircling the church but over the centuries has shifted some ¼ mile east.

Wistow Old Village has long since disappeared but the Hall and St Wistan's Church remain set in splendid parkland. The church and surrounding park attracts many visitors especially at weekends and there is a large garden centre close to the hall. Wistow Hall is private and is basically of Jacobean design although largely rebuilt in the early nineteenth century. Sir Richard Halford bought the Manor House in 1603 and was a great Royalist. It was a great honour when Charles I stayed at Wistow Hall for the evening after the fateful battle of Naseby in 1645 for the Halford family.

Newton Harcourt village is scattered along the banks of the Grand Union Canal but is in the main hidden away from view by the railway cutting. At Newton Top Lock is a beautiful lock keeper's cottage with the lock surrounded by woodland. A picnic table in summer is available outside the lock keeper's cottage for use by walkers or canal users.

Fleckney was known as "Flechenie" in the Domesday Book and at that time was smaller than Wistow. Today, Fleckney is the largest village in the area having expanded over the centuries and is now a popular residential village for commuters to Leicester. The church of St Nicholas is early twelfth century but has no spire or tower. The Old Crown pub makes an excellent half-way stopping off point and is a typical village pub serving bar snacks with a range of "guest" beers.

Footnote

Choose a pleasant sunny day for this walk to experience the rural countryside of South Leicestershire at its finest. The canal section is magical with good views, although slightly disappointing is the low number of narrow boats that use this part of the Leicester line of the Grand Union canal. All footpaths are relatively easy to follow and the path from Fleckney to Kilby is a joy to walk.

Walk 11: Leicester and the Grand Union Canal

Distance: 7 miles

Maps: O.S. Landranger 140, Leicester and Coventry area; O.S. Pathfinder 894 (SK40/50)

Location: Birstall is situated three miles north of Leicester City centre bordered by the A6 and A46 roads. From Redhill roundabout on the A6 turn into Birstall village, then at the next roundabout turn onto Front Street by the Earl of Stamford. Bear left onto Whiles Lane and the walk starts at the Riverside. Grid reference 598092.

Parking: Along Whiles Lane by the River Soar

Refreshments: The White Horse, Birstall – Riverside Pub; The North Bridge Tavern, Leicester – Canalside Pub

Public Transport:

By Rail: Nearest British Rail station is at Leicester

By Bus: Loughborough/Leicester service operated by Kinch Bus. Blaby/Leicester service operated by Midland Fox. (Two bus services are required to return you from Aylestone to Birstall)

Here is a chance to walk along the tow-path and riverside path from Birstall to Aylestone passing right through the city centre of Leicester. The Navigation and River bring greenery and wildlife into the heart of the city and provides a pleasant environment for many sporting activities. Under the Riverside Park scheme Leicester City Council have completed a programme of access, information boards, and footpath improvements giving the opportunity for all who live in the urban city jungle to enjoy the benefits of rural life.

The Route

A gate gives access to the River Soar footpath on your right where Whiles Lane runs adjacent to the river. Follow the narrow path

The bridge over Birstall lock

ahead and to the right of a footbridge is the White Horse pub that sells traditional ales and has hot and cold food available. This late eighteenth-century inn originally had a coal wharf where barges brought their loads as the landlord of the White Horse was also a local coal merchant. At Birstall lock cross over the lock bridge and turn right along the opposite bank of the river where to your left is the start of Watermead Ecological Park. Opened in 1970, this has developed into a mature nature reserve with birds such as redshank, reed bunting, lapwing, and numerous species of water fowl all to be seen along with many other different types of feathered creatures.

Sweep right over the long footbridge that bridges the weir to follow the meandering riverside path for one mile before passing beneath the A5131 Watermead Way road bridge. Ignore the cycle way and continue along the riverside path and in due course a former boundary post marked 'Parish of Thurmaston – City of Leicester, 1891' will be reached.

The next boundary post indicates that you have joined the Riverside Park tow path and a plaque states that Councillor Grundy, Chairman of the Planning Committee, opened the park in September

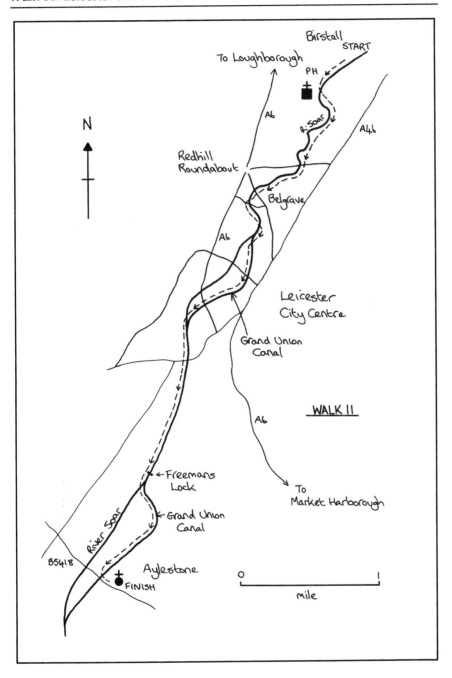

1987. Away to the right is Leicester Outdoor Pursuits Centre and after passing beneath Loughborough Road Bridge, number 13, the riverside path is well-waymarked with Riverside Park posts and arrows. At Thurcaston Road Bridge, leave the river and cross over to rejoin the riverside path on the opposite bank and enter the beautiful Abbey Watermeadows Parkland.

Cross Holden Street Bridge, which is an attractive cable-stayed footbridge replacing an earlier bridge, and was officially opened on 27th September 1985. Walk along the water's edge to Belgrave Lock and here the River Soar curls off to the right into Abbey Park. Cross over Swans Nest footbridge noting an extremely large weir adjacent to Belgrave Lock, and now follow the tow path of the Grand Union Canal on the right. This part of the canal is extremely wide and somewhat untidy reflecting the industrial area that you are now walking through. At Belgrave Gate pass beneath the road and here are the remnants of the old wharf where dye works and hosiery once flourished.

Lime Kiln Lock is 4' 3" deep and an information board describes the area with its history. An interesting plaque by the lock gives mileages by waterway to various cities in Britain and overlooking the canal is the tall building of Epic House which houses on the eighth floor the popular BBC Radio Leicester local radio station. A tow path from the lock is tree-lined while opposite are more warehouses and derelict buildings – quite a contrast!

Pass St Margaret's Pasture Sports Centre where there is an all purpose astro turf sports pitch, then pass beneath the modern St Margaret's Way. This new road has replaced Pasture Bridge and once the Great Central Railway crossed the riverside west of this point. Hosiery, dye and bleach works once crowded the canalside and other industries such as bone line plaster, and cement works would be found within easy reach of the canal. As you walk along the tow path now it will be seen that riverside is no longer just another industrial backwater but with careful observation much of the history of Leicester's canal is evident.

At Bowmans Lane you many fancy calling at the North Bridge Tavern for refreshments but if not continue past North Lock then sweep round to the left by crossing a long footbridge to Soar Lane Island. This is a man-made island created with the building of the Leicester Navigation canal and the areas around the island became an important transfer point for carrying coal to London when the Leicester and Swannington railway was opened in 1832. Pass beneath Soar Lane Bridge, built in 1879, noting the colourful ornate bridges around the island. Another long footbridge brings you to the point where Soar and Union meet again and go beneath Frog Island Road Bridge to reach West Bridge.

From West Bridge, walk along the "Mile Straight" by Western Boulevard which is crossed by many ornamental iron bridges. An interesting point to note is that all the riverside sign posts indicate the next bridge or place in minutes, rather than distance. Over to the left is Leicester City Football Club, with its magnificent new stand, just before reaching Freeman's Lock. Here the River Soar was widened as part of Leicester Corporation's flood prevention measures, when the lock was constructed about 1890, and now hosts the annual rowing regatta. Walk past the extremely large unprotected weir, where the River Soar and Grand Union separate, and the weir bottom seems very popular with anglers.

After passing beneath the Leicester – Burton Upon Trent freight only railway line follow canal signs for Aylestone 1½ miles. At St Mary's Mill Lock is the large gas holder of Aylestone Gas Works and, after the next bridge, bear left to Aylestone Mill. The water now returns to a more canal-like appearance. After Aylestone Mill Bridge, number 108, ignore signs for the Great Central Way. Pass Aylestone Mill Lock to reach Aylestone Meadows nature reserve where information boards are placed along the canal detailing the habitat of the Meadows.

Between bridge 107, Parsons Bridge, and 106, Freestone Bridge, the canal passes some beautiful canalside gardens and the church of Aylestone is seen to the left. Leave the canal at bridge 106 and turn left onto Middleton Street and in about ¼ mile St Andrews church will be reached and a bus stop, where buses run frequently back to the City of Leicester.

Points of Interest

Belgrave Hall, Thurcaston Road is a small Queen Ann house of 1709-1713 with period rooms from the late seventeenth to the mid-nineteenth century. There are outstanding gardens with over 6,500 species of plants. Open all year and admission is free.

Leicestershire Museum of Technology, Corporation Street, is located in the former Victorian Abbey Pumping Station which was built in 1891. The main attraction is the original giant beam engines built by Gimson of Leicester. Beam engines are in steam on certain weekends and there is a fine transport collection. Open all year, with free admission except when special events are taking place.

Abbey Park has remained relevantly undisturbed for the last 100 years by the Leicester developers although trams have come and gone from Abbey Park Road. A popular park with local people it contains many areas of leisure interest and boat trips on the River Soar aboard the cruiser Duke of Bridgewater are available every Sunday during summer from the Waterside Centre. There is no longer an abbey in the park, as it was dissolved at the Reformation. The building was converted into a large mansion but was then demolished during the Civil War. In 1530 Cardinal Wolsey died and was buried at the Abbey. The park is open daily with no admission charge.

Magazine Gateway was once used for the storage of arms but now houses the Museum of the Royal Leicestershire Regiment. Open all year, admission is free except for special events.

Leicester Guildhall was built around 1390 and during the reign of Henry VII became the Town Hall until the new Town Hall was built in 1876. It is well worth a visit and look out for the nineteenth-century police cells, a far cry from today's modern cells.

Jewry Wall Museum, off St Nicholas Circle traces Leicester history from pre-historic times to the Middle Ages. By the museum is the second-century Roman Wall and excavated Roman Bath sites for viewing with a very small portion of the wall remaining. Open all year except for Fridays, admission is free.

Footnote

Leicester is rich in history and museums. As you follow the canal through the city any of the places mentioned above are very easy to walk to but it is a good idea that you have about your person a Leicester street plan just in case you get lost. My points of interest list are nowhere near exhaustive and many other museums are worthy of a visit.

Walk 12: Wanlip and the Grand Union Canal

Distance: 3 miles

Maps: O.S. Landranger 129, Nottingham and Loughborough area; O.S. Landranger 140, Leicester and Coventry area; O.S. Pathfinder 875 (SK61/71); O.S. Pathfinder 895 (SK60/70).

Location: Wanlip sits in the lower half of a letter 'H' banded by the A6, A46 and B673 roads, six miles north of Leicester. From the A6 road go along the B673 Wanlip Road to Syston, crossing the River Soar at Pochin's Bridge. Turn right into Watermead Country Park where a track leads to the car park at King Lear's Lake. Grid reference 606105.

Parking: Free car park, King Lear's Lake, Watermead Country Park.

Refreshments: Hope and Anchor, Wanlip Road, Syston – by canalside.

Public Transport:

> **By Rail:** Nearest British Rail station is at Syston
>
> **By Bus:** Leicester/Loughborough service passes entrance to Country Park on Wanlip Road – Kinch Bus only.

A short circular route that never strays very far from canal, river or lake. Watermead Country Park is relatively modern but the ecology of the area appears to have become established extremely quickly. Ornithologists will gain immense satisfaction from the walk as numerous species of birds will be observed in their normal habitat. It has been known for short-eared owls to nest in the private nature reserve, much to the delight of the local twitchers.

The Route

Before setting off on this ecological walk stop, look, and listen and you be amazed by the different sounds that fill the air. Perhaps a cuckoo in the distance will be heard, or a magpie chatting to itself, the warbling of a skylark overhead, or the pleasant song of a linnet.

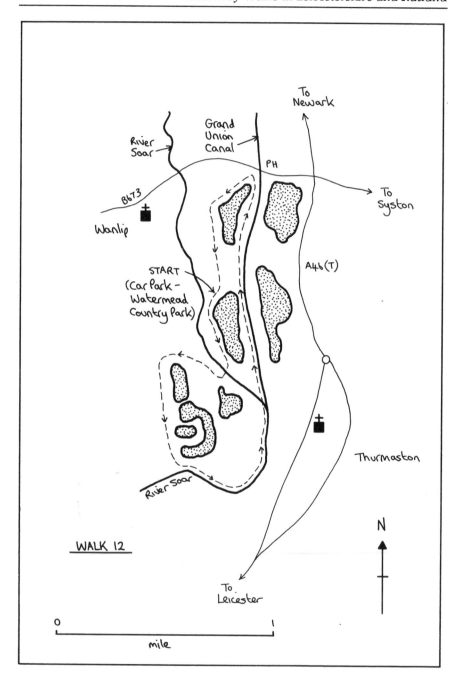

To Newark

Grand Union Canal

River Soar

PH

B673

Wanlip

To Syston

START
(Car Park -
Watermead
Country Park)

A46 (T)

River Soar

Thurmaston

WALK 12

River Soar

To Leicester

N

O | mile

Special guided walks are available at selected times of the year around the country park and one not to be missed is the "Dawn Chorus at Watermead Country Park". For anyone interested there is a start time of 5.00 a.m. and details may be obtained from Leicestershire Rural Community Council (part of Leicestershire County Council) where a special leaflet is available.

Walk through the entrance gate to King Lear's Lake and turn right onto a newly-constructed lakeside path. This is the largest lake in the Country Park and is popular with local sail-boarders. If it is windy day the lake will be a colourful mass of sail-boards. Nearby, on the right is the River Soar; this part of the river is not frequently walked and makes an ideal home for plant and animal life. Listen carefully and you may hear the squeaking of field voles and shrews or other small rodents. At the far end of the lake you pass a monument depicting a scene from William Shakespeare's play "King Lear," which is a feature of the Country Park.

King Lear's Lake

Turn right at a signpost for Birstall ¾ mile and cross over the River Soar bridge to reach a second signpost. Turn right in the direction of Wanlip ¾ mile and follow the country path looking out at all times for riders on mountain bikes. The park appears to encourage the pursuit of mountain bike riding along the smooth wide paths and tracks. A smaller lakeside path is now evident and in due course swings to the left. Continue ahead along this path, and in places it passes through pretty woodland, before reaching the alternative entrance to the park at Meadow Lane, Birstall. Climb two stiles in quick succession adjacent to the small car park then pass through a short section of beautiful woodland to the right. Bear right at a junction of paths and very quickly the end of the Country Park is reached.

Turn left onto the footpath of the River Soar, then join a grassy path that runs adjacent to the river. The path now snakes around the edge of Watermead Country Park for about ¼ mile and is never far from the edge of the river. Eventually the weir by Thurmaston Lock is passed and a footpath for Thurmaston must be ignored as this will only lead you to the village. Continue ahead in the direction of Wanlip as indicated on the public footpath sign noting to your left a hopper where gravel extraction is taking place. Climb an unusual shaped stile and join a grassy path for a short distance, then cross over a footbridge that spans a weir and the River Soar. From here you are now following the Grand Union Canal and all entrances into the Country Park from the canal are to be ignored. The tow path is idyllic and a mature hedge on the left gives privacy from the neighbouring Country Park. Over to the right is Wanlip Country Club and lake where speed boats cut through the water with a skier in tow. From this charming part of the Grand Union Canal the church of Wanlip can be seen in the distance to the left.

A most unusual occurrence during the week takes place on the canal just north of Thurmaston. Two barges are harnessed together and transport gravel from the hopper that was passed earlier near Thurmaston Lock to the cement plant at Syston owned by Ennemix. The barges belong to British Waterways but sub contract to Ennemix and chug up and down the canal all day. At weekends the barges will be found stabled by the cement plant. Just before the B673 road bridge turn left through the gate to enter the Country Park. However, if you fancy some light refreshments continue to the road and cross to the Hope and Anchor pub opposite.

Follow the track round a small lake to the right then go along a thin path before joining the access track back to the car park at King Lear's Lake. There is just time to enjoy further views of sailing boats on the lake that heralds the end of this short but educational and recreational walk.

Points of Interest

Watermead Country Park, Syston is in 230 acres of former gravel pit workings and is bounded by the Grand Union Canal and River Soar. Many of the gravel pits have been flooded and developed into attractive lakes with a variety of water sports taking place on them especially at weekends. Although the Country Park is still evolving there are many beautiful lakeside woodland paths, picnic areas, nature reserves and even a "hide" to discover. One of the oldest lakes, known locally as Jelson's Lake, is over 50 years old and is seen when entering the Country Park from the alternative entrance at Meadow Lane, Birstall.

Wanlip is a small hamlet of some 184 inhabitants and although still remote the parish is getting closer to Birstall by the day. The thirteenth-century church there is famous for having the first English inscription on a brass in the country.

Birstall can only be described as a village with the population of a small town. Its history stretches back to a Saxon settlement, some 1300 years ago, and the old English name of "Burh Steall" means " the old disused fort." Birstall is mainly a commuter village for business men working in Leicester and its appearance has changed dramatically during this century. However, tucked away in the old part of the village one or two timber framed cottages remain and, in the church of St James, look out for the "Birstall Beast", a stone carving of a unidentified animal, found within the last 50 years.

Thurmaston has very little to offer in historic content other than the church of St Michael. Restored in 1848, the perpendicular tower was left untouched, the north and south arcades are circa 1300. However, a recent discovery of an Anglo-Saxon burial cemetery has linked the village with Roman Britain.

Footnote

The saying 'good things come in small packages' can be applied to the walk. The Country Park is a place to linger and is the only water park in Leicestershire to have such a wide variety of habitat available at all times to the general public for exploration. An ideal family walk where young children can learn about nature at 'grass roots' level and spend as much time as required. At the end of the canal walk is the Hope and Anchor pub, where a drink or refreshments should be experience on the open-air terrace.

Walk 13: Cossington and the River Soar

Distance: 6 miles

Maps: O.S. Landranger 129, Nottingham and Loughborough area; O.S. Pathfinder 874 (SK41/51); O.S. Pathfinder 875 (SK61/71)

Location: Cossington stands on flat ground between the River Wreake and the River Soar close the A46(T) road. The city of Leicester is about six miles to the south. If approaching along the A6 by-pass road turn right onto the B5328 road to Sileby and Cossington is located one mile along the road. The walk commences from All Saints Parish Church on Main Street. Grid reference 604137.

Parking: Roadside parking in village only.

Refreshments: Free Trade Inn, Sileby. Refreshment shop at Sileby Mill and Lock. A coffee shop is open in the Old Mill.

Public Transport:

By Rail: Nearest British Rail station is at Sileby or Syston.

By Bus: Leicester/Loughborough service via Sileby operated by Kinch Bus.

Here is an open countryside and riverside walk from a village that is one of the prettiest in Charnwood. Cossington has a mixture of old and new houses with many cottages having thatched roofs. Over half of the route follows the River Wreake, the Grand Union Canal, and River Soar and calls at two old water mills now restored as a restaurant and a residential house. The Free Trade Inn on Cossington Road, Sileby, is believed to be 500 years old and is very much the traditional English wayside pub, which makes an ideal stopping-off point.

The Route

Before embarking onto the walk the area around the church is purely delightful and must be investigated. The church is half hidden in trees and entrance to the churchyard is through the metal kissing gates. Around the War Memorial are a number of half-timbered thatched roof cottages and in this quaint area of Cossington time seems to have stood still.

With the church of All Saints on your right walk along Main Street for 100 yards as far as Bennetts Lane and turn left, then at Back Lane a public footpath sign is found. A long straight field path runs parallel with the Midland Main Line Railway and after crossing a minor road continue ahead in the same course over two more fields to the right of The Chestnuts Farm to reach the embankment of the A46(T) road.

Go through the tunnel beneath the road into a rough pasture field and your destination now is a stile to the right. A short grassy path returns back under the A46(T) road and here you are able to pick up the footpath by the edge of the River Wreake. Exercise caution along the river bank as the path follows extremely close to the water's edge and in summer becomes quite overgrown.

Where the River Wreake flows into the Grand Union Canal is a magnificent wooden footbridge, but this must not be crossed; instead continue ahead on the same bank, following the canal and passing the weir to your left. This area seems very popular with Canada geese as the fields around the overflow weir contains many flocks of these excitable creatures. At Junction Lock there is a change in water level of four feet nine inches and the views from this section of the canal are not very appealing to the eye. The land is scarred from sand and gravel extraction and in places is a blot on the landscape, but much remedial work has been carried out by the owners and no doubt in time the old gravel pits will be transformed into lakes and areas of natural beauty.

The River Soar rejoins the canal just before you cross a footbridge near to Cossington Mill and a little further ahead is a view of the weir by the Mill. At Cossington Lock, join the B5328 road and opposite the entrance to the Mill Restaurant, turn left at a public footpath sign for Sileby Mill. A difficult path descends to a stile where a waymark arrow shows the way. Very quickly the footpath hugs the contours of the River Soar and stiles need to be climbed intermittently. As you journey along the river the land around is flat and there are good views of the villages of Sileby and Cossington. The church at Sileby stands proud and has a commanding view of

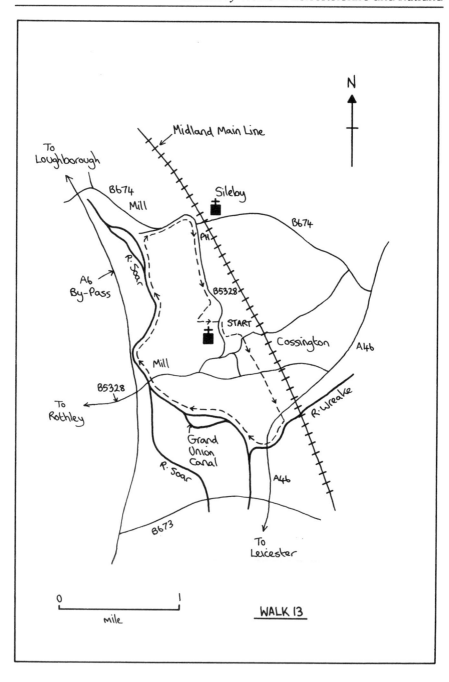

WALK 13

the Soar Valley. A footpath joins from the right and from here to Sileby Mill, a mile away, the riverside path becomes part of the "Leicestershire Round" long distance footpath.

At Sileby Mill do not cross the footbridges over the weir and River Soar but continue to a stile that leads out onto Mill Lane. Turn right past the mill building and boatyard to reach a road junction. Go through a kissing gate where a footpath cuts across several fields to the right of Sileby church to the B5328 road. Turn right along the road and in short distance is The Free Trade Inn, an Everards pub, with a thatched roof and whitewashed walls. A warm welcome awaits walkers although muddy boots may have to be removed. Follow Cossington Road out of Sileby and after ¾ mile turn right at a double stile. A pleasant field path now returns you to the left-hand side of the church and a kissing gate gives access to the lane by the war memorial and churchyard.

Points of Interest

Cossington is a small friendly village noted for several half-timbered thatched cottages. Magpie cottage, circa 1584, is probably the oldest cottage in the village and is located by the War Memorial at the start of the walk. Thirteenth-century All Saints Parish Church has many interesting features, especially the stained glass window, and is worth looking around.

Cossington Mill, Weir and Lock lie one mile west of the village and from the tow path by the lock there is a fine view of the former corn mill. Records show that the present mill has stood since 1284 on its current site but a mill has been noted at Cossington for much longer. The mill is now a very exclusive restaurant with high quality meals served against the backcloth of the River Soar.

Sileby Mill, Lock, and Boatyard is a haven for boaters and colourful narrowboats are passing through the lock or mooring at the river basin during all parts of the day. The mill is less interesting than Cossington Mill and drab in comparison. Having been used for many years as a leather board factory it has recently been converted to a house and it is hoped that one day a coffee shop will be opened on the ground floor of the mill.

Sileby Village is recorded in the Domesday Book of 1086 but the civilisation is much older as it is known that in the late ninth century after the Danes invaded Britain Sileby became a Danish settlement. Like many other villages in this area during the nineteenth century framework knitting abounded along with a boot and shoe industry. The early 1900s saw Sileby boasting a brewery, a gas works next door, several brick works, and boot and shoe manufacturers. Today's industry, is very different with small engineering units replacing the large factory industries. The church of St Mary's dates back in parts to 1152 with extras added up to about 1450 and dominates the village. It has been described as "the cathedral of the Soar Valley".

Sileby Mill: now a block of a residential house overlooking the River Soar

Footnote

All footpaths and riverside tow paths are clear to walk although the path to the River Wreake either side of the A46(T) road is not waymarked. Part of the walk follows the "Leicestershire Round", a 100-mile circular walk around Leicestershire that begins at Burrough Hill near Melton Mowbray. Take time to enjoy the many riverside views and do stay for a while at Sileby Lock to watch the boating activities in the lock and basin.

Walk 14: Mountsorrel and The River Soar

Distance: 5 miles

Maps: O.S. Landranger 129, Nottingham and Loughborough area; O.S. Pathfinder 874 (SK41/51)

Location: Mountsorrel is four miles to the south of Loughborough and seven miles north of Leicester clustered around the A6 road. With the opening of the A6 by-pass road the village has once more returned to peace and tranquillity that has not been known for many years. From the A6 road turn onto the B674 road to Sileby where the Waterside Inn is found 100 yards on the right. The walk starts at Mountsorrel Lock opposite the public house. Grid reference 583154.

Parking: Free car parking in Mountsorrel on the A6 road by the memorial hall.

Refreshments: Many excellent pubs along the route but especially the Waterside Inn, Mountsorrel Lock and the Riverside Inn, Barrow upon Soar.

Public Transport:

By Rail: Nearest British Rail station is at Sileby

By Bus: Leicester/Loughborough frequent service operated by Midland Fox and Kinch Bus.

This walk is tailor-made for anyone who appreciates a waterside stroll coupled with lock-side pubs. Between Mountsorrel and Quordon the River Soar curls first one way then the other, passing through lush green meadows before curving around to Barrow upon Soar. In fact, at Barrow upon Soar there is a short stretch of Grand Union canal that by-passes the meandering river which is extremely graceful with trees lining the edge of both banks. The boatyard, marina, locks and public houses of these three villages combine to make this, one of the most colourful sections of river to examine and enjoy.

The weir at Mountsorrel

The Route

Parking is difficult around the Waterside Inn so it is best that the free car park on the A6 road in Mountsorrel is used. This will also give the opportunity to inspect the Butter Cross, a domed and Tuscan columned structure built around 1793, which is only a short distance away from the pub.

A stile will be noticed on the road bridge opposite Mountsorrel Lock and after a short stretch of grass a second stile gives access to a water meadow path. From here is an excellent view of the three sided weir and river basin and is a most picturesque spot. Pass beneath the red bricked bridge built in 1860 to enable the quarries in Mountsorrel to transport granite by rail over the river to the railway siding at Barrow upon Soar, a distance of two miles away. Before the coming of the railway, river boats were loaded with stone and dispatched northwards to the River Trent. In the late 1970s, a continuous conveyor belt replaced the rail wagons and shunting engines. Today granite chippings are sent along a mechanised roller structure to Barrow upon Soar which accounts for a third of all Redland Aggregates sales.

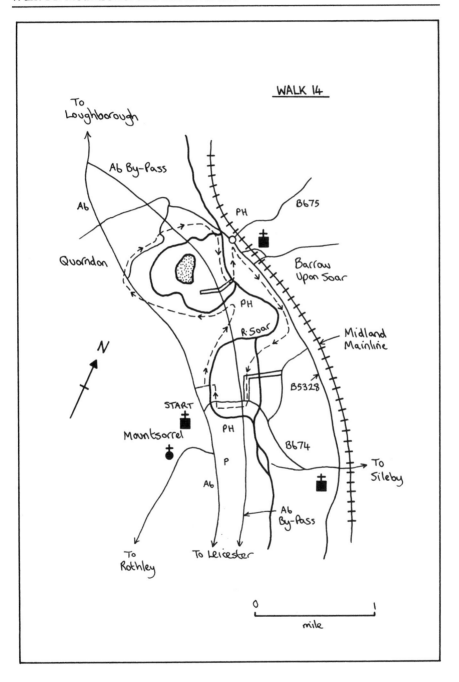

At the footbridge cross over to the opposite bank and continue ahead passing many colourful narrowboats moored along this section of the river. Keep an eye open for many types of water birds such as moorhens, teals, and mallard ducks swimming and diving in the fast flowing river. In due course go through a small tunnel then walk parallel to the A6 by-pass for about 100 yards to a stile where another longer tunnel goes beneath the road. Cross a field to the river and stile, but do not climb the stile, instead turn back on yourself and follow the riverside path to the A6 by-pass road. Once under the road the riverside footpath is obvious to walk along and as progress is made over the green water meadow fields there are many fine views to saviour.

Upon reaching the A6 road turn right into Quorn village and after passing Quorn village hall, built in 1889, turn right along School Lane. Ignore the footbridge on Soar Road and join Meynell Road as far as Quorn Hall and turn right. The footpath here has been replaced by a gigantic footbridge over the A6 by-pass and from the bridge an interesting view of Quorn hall, now an outdoor pursuit centre, may be enjoyed. A paved path leads through a line of horse chestnut trees to the B675 road by a three-arched bridge. At this point the River Soar and Grand Union Canal separate and opposite the Riverside Pub is a track that leads to Barrow Lock Bridge, number 29. Turn left along the tow path passing Barrow Deep Lock, some nine feet seven inches in depth, and the moorings. The canal tow path is most beautiful with trees lining both sides of the water's edge and in summer months this is a most popular path with walkers. All too soon the canal has to be left at Mill Lane Bridge, number 28 by the Navigation Inn and from here Mill Lane is taken to the B5328 road in Barrow upon Soar.

Walk along the road to the right through the pleasant village and after about ½ mile there is an alleyway opposite Pingle Nook. At the entrance of Meadow Farm marina and touring caravan park climb a stile and follow the footpath through the park crossing the marina bridge. A stile gives access to a field path, then cross over the River Soar to reach the granite conveyor belt and a kissing gate. Pass through the kissing gate and for the next 50 yards you will have to squeeze alongside the conveyor belt before emerging out into a field. The field perimeter path leads to the A6 by-pass road ignoring a stile on your right. Join a track and follow this to its natural conclusion and turn right along the B675 road where the end of the walk is in sight. Pass beneath the A6 by-pass for the last time and the Waterside Inn will be reached shortly after.

Points of Interest

Mountsorrel is a small town that straddles the A6 road and is perched on the west bank of the River Soar. A castle once overlooked the village but both the castle and the hill that it stood on have long since disappeared. The latter was extensively quarried for red granite and for more than 200 years stone has been worked with many fine examples of Mountsorrel granite being seen in the older buildings of the town.

Quordon or Quorn as it is better known has many fine buildings including the seventeenth-century Quorn Hall and eighteenth-century Bulls Head Inn on the A6 road. Quorn is famous for the fact that it gave its name to probably the finest hunt in Britain where The Hunts founder, Hugho Meynell, lived at Quorn Hall around 1750 bringing his own hounds to the hall from Great Bowden. There are many streets and cottages named after "Meynell" in Quorn especially near to the Hall. Many other street names have connections with hunting.

Barrow upon Soar has two very good riverside pubs both popular with locals and visitors. The thirteenth-century church was virtually rebuilt between 1862 and 1870 but some original features survive and is worth visiting.

Footnote

An ideal family walk with plenty to see. The new A6 by-pass has slightly spoilt the countryside with some footpaths having been diverted. However, waymark arrows and marker posts have been placed in profusion and the line of the original footpaths are soon found. Families will be interested in visiting Stonehurst Family Farm and Museum in Mountsorrel where there is farm trail, tea shop, farm shop, and museum as well as a "cuddle corner" where children can handle small animals.

Walk 15: Loughborough and the Grand Union Canal

Distance: 7 miles

Maps: O.S. Landranger 129, Nottingham and Loughborough area; O.S. Pathfinder 874 (SK41/51)

Location: The University Town of Loughborough is bisected by the A6 road and is easily accessible by the M1 from Leicester or Nottingham. A short walk from the town centre, Loughborough Central Station on Great Central Road is well-signposted or alternatively from the British Rail Station it is as equally as close. Grid reference 545194.

Parking: Street parking along Great Central Road adjacent to Loughborough Central Railway Station.

Refreshments: The Griffin Inn, Swithland (Good Food). Buffet at Great Central Railway, Loughborough Central Station.

Public Transport:

By Rail: Nearest British Rail station is at Loughborough

By Bus: Leicester/Loughborough/Derby services operated by various bus companies including Kinch Bus and Midland Fox Bus.

A linear walk commencing from the headquarters of the Great Central Railway at Loughborough Central Station that recaptures the ambience of an earlier time. Soak up the rich fragrance of canal life along the Grand Union Canal, then taste the smell of steam from Britain's only preserved mainline railway as you follow the line to the Victorian Station at Rothley. Return in style by steam train to enjoy the views of Charnwood and especially of Swithland Reservoir which is bridged by the railway line.

The Route

Within 400 yards of each other are two rival forms of transport separated by 100 years. The Grand Union Canal arrived first in

A steam train on the Great Central Railway crossing Swithland viaduct

Loughborough in 1794 to be superseded by the Great Central Railway opened in 1899. In the 1950s the motor car had a serious effect on the railways and this line was closed altogether in 1966; gladly, both modes of transport survive today.

From the station on your left walk along Great Central Road to Moor Lane and the canal bridge to join the tow path to the right. Very soon the buildings are left behind and the canal bends to the left by the moorings of the Peter le Marchant Trust. Cross the long narrow bridge over the overflow and follow the tow path ahead passing beneath Millers Bridge, number 34. The canal winds through rural countryside known as Loughborough moors to reach Woodthorpe Bridge, where the canal is now left.

Cross over the bridge onto a track and follow for about a mile to the A6 road at the Bull in the Hollow Farm. Take care in crossing the dual carriageway to Woodthorpe Road opposite and the first sighting of the Great Central Railway. After a ¼ mile turn left at a public footpath sign for Quordon, and a track leads back over the railway to a small wood. Skirt round One Ash Wood to the right, then follow a stream to the B591 road and a kissing gate opposite in

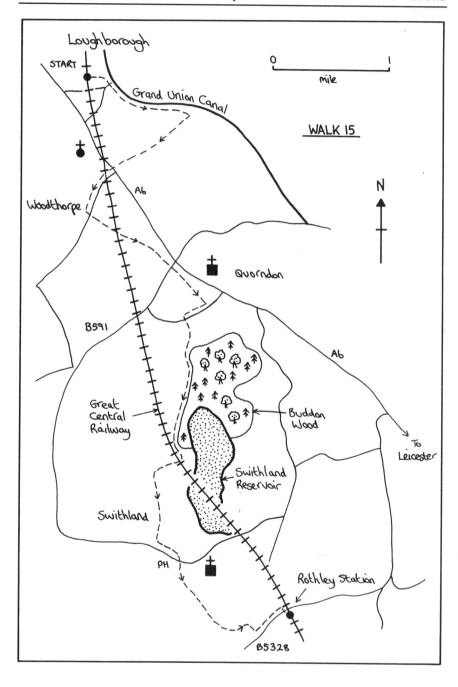

Quorndon. From here a narrow path weaves through scrub land at the back of a housing estate and in summer this path becomes overgrown but is quite passable. Turn right along an alleyway, then left by the cricket club into Spinney drive to the junction with Chaveney Road. About 200 yards to the right is Mill Farm and a public footpath sign.

At the end of the lane a stile gives access to a very pleasant waterside path by a stream. On the left is Buddon Wood, and at a point where the steam bears to the left climb a half hidden stile. An obvious field path brings you to the outer perimeter of Swithland Reservoir and the path now threads itself round the iron fence of the reservoir gardens. On rare occasions Severn Trent Water open up the beautiful gardens for public inspection. At Kinchley Lane cross over the railway bridge and turn left at a public footpath sign. A very obvious field perimeter path is taken over the next two fields towards Swithland. Look out for a muddy lane and tread carefully as cattle constantly use the right of way between the two gates. Follow the lane now for a short distance which brings you to the road in Swithland village.

Turn left and walk through the village noting many fine thatched cottages and expensive houses. The Griffin Inn on the right was the Griffin Hotel, built in the late nineteenth century as a coaching house; it serves traditional ales and is the ideal place to stop for refreshments. Fifty yards past the inn, turn right at a public bridleway sign and walk along the track to a stile. Cross the rough pasture field to the left enjoying a superb view of Swithland Hall then pass through a small wood to emerge out onto a field path. Away in the distance to the right is Old John Folly standing proud on a hill in Bradgate Park and from here follow the field perimeter path over a number of fields to reach an obvious turn to the left onto another footpath. Shortly, turn right over a stream where a track leads up hill to a gate and the road. Turn left along the B5330 road for ½ mile to reach Rothley station and the Great Central Railway.

Points of Interest

Loughborough is the largest town in the county next to the city of Leicester and is a thriving town along the River Soar. On 5th July 1841 Thomas Cook organised the world's first railway excursion from Leicester to Loughborough conveying 570 passengers at a fare of one shilling to attend a temperance rally. A unique feature to Loughborough is the yearly street fun fair held for three days in early November that dates back to the reign of Henry VIII.

The Great Central Railway extends for seven miles from Loughborough to Birstall (Leicester North) and operates steam services throughout the year. The preserved railway is the only line in Britain to have mainline status and gives you the opportunity to re-live those steam days again or for the first time. Loughborough Central Station, museum, and engine shed are worthy of inspection and during recent years the line has formed the perfect backcloth for films and television programmes depicting an earlier age.

Swithland is famous for its slate quarries although production of slate ceased in the late nineteenth century. There is a slate monument in the churchyard of St Leonard's Church which stands as a tribute to the slate industry.

Rothley is a large village with thatched cottages spread around the green. The churchyard is a ninth-century Saxon cross and the church of St Mary and St John the Baptist is most impressive. The Victorian railway station is extremely authentic with gas lights in use for the lighting. A small refreshment room is available on the platform by the ticket office.

Footnote

During the summer months the Great Central Railway operates a frequent service, but more infrequent during the winter. A timetable and information leaflet is available and it is recommended that you telephone 01509 230726 beforehand to confirm train departure times from Rothley Station.

Walk 16: Stanford on Soar and The River Soar

Distance: 7 miles

Maps: O.S. Landranger 129, Nottingham and Loughborough area; O.S. Pathfinder 853 (SK42/52)

Location: Stanford on Soar is located between the A60 and A6006 roads two miles north of Loughborough on the Leicestershire and Nottinghamshire county border. The walk commences from the Church of St John the Baptist. Grid reference 544221.

Parking: Small car park for church may be used except on Sundays, otherwise where possible in the village.

Refreshments: The Boat Inn and the Albion Inn, Loughborough – both by the canal side. The Plough Inn, Normanton on Soar – riverside.

Public Transport:

By Rail: Nearest British Rail station is at Loughborough

By Bus: A daily service between Nottingham/Loughborough operated by South Notts Buses.

Here is a refreshing walk that encompasses the River Soar and the Grand Union Canal through Loughborough. There are many surprising panoramic views over Charnwood, the Leicestershire Wolds and Rushcliffe. The two border villages visited of Stanford on Soar and Normanton on Soar are positively charming and a delight to explore. With a choice of three super pubs along the way, allow plenty of time to drink in the variety that is on offer.

The Route

The church car park may be used for parking in Stanford on Soar except on Sundays as it is constantly in use for church services in mornings and evenings. A notice is displayed to this effect and the local congregation are liable to park around your car, possibly blocking you in if you ignore this request.

Walk along the road for 200 yards towards East Leake to a public footpath sign and stile and turn left on to a field footpath. At the end of this field turn right and cross a succession of stiles to the former Great Central Railway Line. The disused track is still in place, now very rusty, but it is hoped that one day the main line steam trust will be able to extend the private line from Loughborough to Ruddington. After crossing the line an obvious footpath now climbs Fox Hill and below there is a superb view of the River Soar meandering through the open countryside.

The thin footpath now descends to the River Soar and it is likely that small groups of cattle will be grazing in these fields close to the path. They are friendly but inquisitive and if you have a dog with you it is advisable to have your dog on a leash. After ½ mile the path swings away from the river to the Midland Mainline Railway and extreme care must be taken when crossing the four tracks as this is not a boarded crossing. Please ensure that you look both ways as high speed trains thunder along these tracks. Turn right by a stream and walk ahead to the road where a grassy verge should be followed into the peaceful village of Normanton on Soar.

In the village is the Plough Inn, a half-timbered pub with a beautiful riverside garden, which makes a fine stopping off point for liquid refreshments and serves excellent lunches. Where the road bends sharply to the right, turn left at a public footpath sign and follow the field path over these fields to the A6006 road at Zouch and turn left.

Cross over Zouch Bridge, number 43, then descend to a long footbridge that spans the weir. After crossing two more smaller footbridges access is gained to the riverside path. Vast sums of money has been spent by British Waterways to cure the problems of flooding along the Soar valley and it appears that the alterations at Zouch have been a success. The riverside path back to Normanton on Soar is idyllic with chalets and immaculately kept gardens along the opposite bank reaching down to the water's edge. A number of stiles are interspersed along the path which is extremely easy to follow. In due course the footpath returns to a more typical riverside path and soon after the separating of the River Soar into two the deep lock of Bishop Meadow is reached. Here the water rises by eight feet seven inches and at the next bridge the path crosses to the opposite bank.

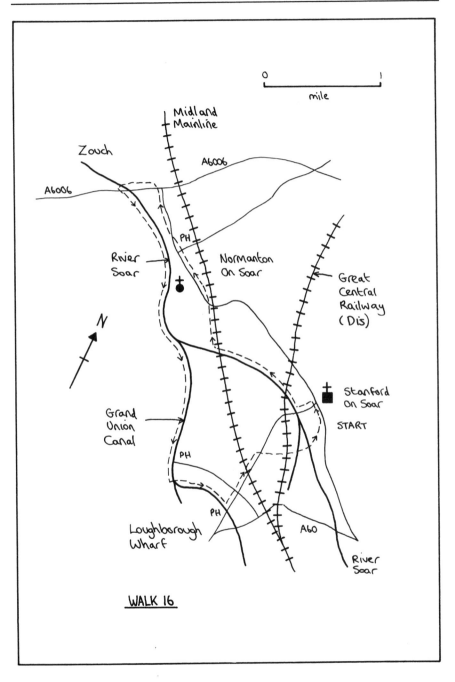

0 _____ 1
mile

Midland Mainline

Zouch

A6006

A6006

River Soar

PH

Normanton On Soar

Great Central Railway (Dis)

N

Grand Union Canal

Stanford On Soar

START

PH

PH

Loughborough Wharf

A60

River Soar

WALK 16

From here onwards the river gives way to the Grand Union Canal and after Loughborough Lock is the Albion Inn. A sharp left turn brings you to the Boat Inn and the end of the waterside walk. Turn left along Meadow Lane and continue ahead over the railway bridge passing the Brush Works to a public footpath sign on the right. An obvious field path leads to the Great Central Railway embankment where a tunnel brings you to two bridges over the River Soar. Cross a short field to the road then turn left along the road back into Stanford on Soar and the church of St John the Baptist.

The Boat Inn, Loughborough: passed on the tow path of the Grand Union Canal

Points of Interest

Stanford on Soar is an extremely small village with very few amenities situated just over the border in Nottinghamshire. The church of St John the Baptist is very photogenic and dates back to the thirteenth century although the splendid tower is fifteenth century. In the base of the tower are blocks of Mountsorrel granite, while on the chancel floor is a brass portrait of a priest, one of only two ecclesiastical brasses in Nottinghamshire.

Normanton on Soar also has a thirteenth-century church with a fine spire. The church of St James is very much in keeping with the village while at 75 Main Street is a cottage that was built in 1454. This is the oldest house in the village by some 100 years and the front is 60 years younger than the remainder of the cottage. Close by are two half-timbered buildings, the Post Office and The Plough Inn, both important to the local community.

Brush Electrical Engineering, Loughborough, better known as 'The Brush', is by far the largest employer in the area and has been at its present site since 1863 alongside the Midland Railway Station. Now owned by the BTR Group, Brush Works has become famous for manufacturing rolling stock and diesel locomotives for export and for British Rail. Most recently the Brush Works have completed a contract for Class 60 Diesel electric locomotives and shuttle trains for the channel tunnel.

Footnote

No problem in following the footpaths, riverside and tow paths, on this walk. All are frequently used throughout the year and are not overgrown during the summer months. If calling at The Plough Inn at Normanton on Soar the riverside garden is recommended. A word of warning: to stop the adventurous mallard ducks from pecking your legs you will have to share your refreshments with them!

Walk 17: Zouch and the River Soar

Distance: 4½ miles

Maps: O.S. Landranger 129, Nottingham and Loughborough area; O.S. Pathfinder 853 (SK42/52)

Location: Zouch straddles the A6006 road to Melton Mowbray just inside the Nottinghamshire border with Leicestershire some four miles north of Loughborough off the A6 road. The walk begins from the car park on A6006 road. Grid reference 504234.

Parking: Free car park in Zouch on A6006 road.

Refreshments: The Kings Head and The Old Plough – Sutton Bonington. The Rose and Crown – Zouch.

Public Transport:

By Rail: Nearest British Rail station is at Loughborough

By Bus: An hourly Nottingham/Loughborough service via Zouch and Sutton Bonington operated by Barton Buses.

Zouch and Sutton Bonington are two small villages nestling in the Soar Valley, situated on the Nottinghamshire side of the River Soar. An area often overlooked by walkers this ramble plots the course of the River Soar as it meanders through lush green meadows below Whatton House. After curving around Devils Elbow, field paths are taken to Sutton Bonington, which has an unusual tale to tell of its origin, then a pleasant country lane and bridleways return you to the picturesque hamlet of Zouch.

The Route

The riverside hamlet of Zouch consists of the old watermill building, a farmhouse, garage, several red brick cottages, and one of the most popular pubs in the area. Quite a feat for a former canal settlement that has barely grown over the years to support a pub with such a flourishing business!

From the car park, cross over the A6006 road to a bridle road sign

A narrowboat at Zouch lock

opposite and pass through a gate into a grazing field. An obvious path leads to a bridge over Zouch cut and after crossing the bridge turn left onto the tow path. Follow the path to Zouch Lock where a stile gives access to the riverside path. Initially the path cuts away to the right but then rejoins the River Soar after about 400 yards.

The next section of path is along a raised grassy bank where a series of stiles need to be climbed. The A6 road and Whatton House are close to you on the opposite side of the river and after about 11/4 miles of extremely pleasant riverside walking the Soar takes an extremely sharp curve to the left. This stretch of water is known as Devils Elbow and seems to be popular expanse of water for many aquatic birds. You may even be lucky enough to see the resident herons that grace this part of the river.

At the White House pub, unfortunately there is no way across to the pub, turn right over a bridge into a field. Follow the obvious field path ahead heading for the spire of Sutton Bonington church. A succession of stiles shows the way over a number of short fields to Soar Lane. Turn right along Soar Lane into the village of Sutton Bonington to a road junction and then right again.

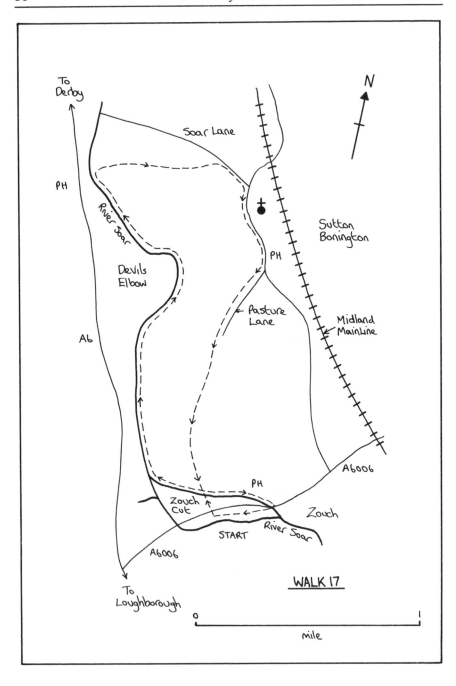

To
Derby

Soar Lane

PH

River Soar

Devils
Elbow

A6

Sutton
Bonington

PH

Pasture
Lane

Midland
MainLine

A6006

PH

Zouch
Cut

Zouch

START

River Soar

A6006

To
Loughborough

WALK 17

N

0   1

mile

As you walk through the village find time to call at the church of St Michael's. The south aisle of the church is thirteenth century, while the spire and upper windows are fifteenth century. If time allows refreshments may be taken at the Kings Head and in 1832 this was one of five public houses to be found in Sutton Bonington. Today the village can boast four. Turn right along Pasture Lane and follow the road to its natural conclusion to join a bridleway. A track then leads into a field where a clear field perimeter path returns you to Zouch Cut and the bridge. Do not cross the bridge, but turn left along the tow path for ½ mile to Zouch basin and the road. Turn right onto the A6006 and further refreshments could be partaken at the Rose and Crown before returning to the car park.

Points of Interest

Zouch Mill existed long before the River Soar became navigable and over the years has been used for a variety of businesses. In 1920 it was turned into a dance-hall and cafe, but more recently has been converted into flats. The Domesday book recorded a mill at Zouch 900 years ago and water still flows underneath the building.

Whatton House was built in 1802 and after a fire restored in 1876. The gardens are open on Sundays between 14.00 hours and 17.00 hours, April to September.

Sutton Bonington was originally two villages, Sutton and Bonington, and over the years both villages expanded and eventually became one. There are still two churches in the village and each church is completely different in character and size with perhaps the little church of St Anne the more interesting. In years gone by the main industries were farming or framework knitting which were worked in the houses of the knitters or in adjacent workshops. The village has many half-timbered houses especially along Soar Lane and in 1993 won the Best Kept Village competition.

Footnote

A personal favourite walk of mine that combines beautiful scenery with a fast flowing river. Well-maintained footpaths and bridleways are the "bread and butter" of this walk. Mix in ingredients such as two historic villages with pleasant pubs and you have the perfect recipe for either an evening cantor or a half day stroll. You will not be disappointed!

Walk 18: Kegworth and the River Soar

Distance: 3½ miles

Maps: O.S. Landranger 129, Nottingham & Loughborough area; O.S. Pathfinder 853 (SK42/52)

Location: Kegworth is six miles north of Loughborough and 11 miles south of Derby on the busy A6 road in North West Leicestershire. From the A6 turn onto Station Road and pass The Anchor Inn to Kegworth Bridge. Grid reference 495272.

Parking: There is no official car park close by; limited parking off the road is available by the bridge.

Refreshments: The Flying Horse and The Anchor Inn – Kegworth. A choice of pubs in Sutton Bonington. (see walk no 17)

Public Transport:

By Rail: Nearest British Rail station is at Loughborough

By Bus: Frequent services operate between Leicester/Loughborough/Derby operated by Barton Buses and Kinch Bus.

Starting from Kegworth Bridge, first impressions will be of trains, boats, and planes. But after crossing the first two fields, an air of peace, tranquillity and bygone days will quickly descend. A good all year round walk, and although modest in length but not in character, it manages to combine beautiful countryside with an idyllic sketch of riverside walking. A line of weeping willow trees sweep down to the water's edge while many other pleasing sights along the River Soar will captivate your interest.

The Route

The Soar Valley is famous for flooding and the land around the River Soar at Kegworth is no exception. To avoid getting wet feet the local authority took the unusual steps to use wooden trestles to raise the pavement level above the road and this appears to have rectified the watery problem. Before you begin the walk from Kegworth Bridge, number 45, it is worth looking back at the handsome nineteenth-century five arch stone bridge specially constructed over the river to cope with the flood water.

By a public footpath sign climb a double stile and accompany the riverside path for a short distance until reaching a line of electricity pylons. Leave the River Soar and cross to a stile opposite on a vague footpath. There is an obvious path to follow over the next field that brings you closer to the Midland Railway line. In a strange sort of way, it is relaxing to watch high speed trains hurtling along the track between London and the North as it leaves you happy in the knowledge that at this moment you are not part of the bustle of everyday life. Pass a pleasant pond known as Black Pool on your left to reach a stream. Cross the double stile either side of the stream and continue ahead to a second double stile. Over to your left is the University of Nottingham's School of Agriculture and experimental farm but, much closer to hand, is Sutton Fields House of a gothic appearance that was prevalent in Western Europe in the twelfth to sixteenth centuries.

Go through a metal kissing gate where a tree-lined path brings you to a track and another kissing gate. A notice warns dog owners to keep their dog on a lead as you continue ahead with a hedge to your left. The church of Sutton Bonington is ahead of you now as you pass through a third metal kissing gate to quickly reach a wooden gate and Soar Lane at the North end of Sutton Bonington village.

300 yards along this lane to the right is a public footpath sign by a stream. An obvious field path leads the way from a stile and it is extremely easy to follow the path crossing a succession of stiles. The River Soar will be seen in the distance and as you walk over the lush green meadows keep your eyes peeled for hares and rabbits darting from hedge to hedge or a kestrel hovering overhead ready to pounce on a unsuspecting rabbit.

Cross a bridge and turn right onto the footpath along side the River Soar opposite The White House pub and restaurant located on the A6. On the far bank, a line of weeping willows sweep down to the water's edge that sets the scene for a waterway walk of exceptional beauty. Water birds such as mallards, coots, moorhens, tufted ducks and swans all frequent these waters and tucked away in the trees on

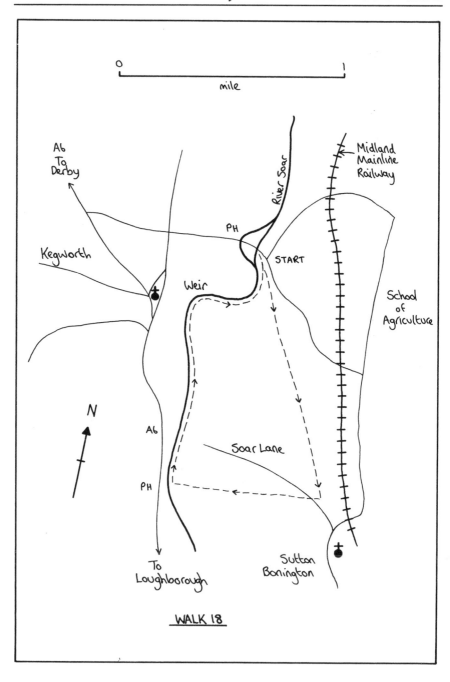

WALK 18

The White House near Kegworth, seen from the River Soar.

the opposite bank is an old mansion with tailored lawns that evokes memories of a bygone age. It is good to see that this old house has now been fully restored to its former glory after suffering considerable fire damage a few years ago. There is no mistaking the sound of a weir as you approach Kegworth deep lock, the noise is quite deafening. The weir is situated in the loop of the river and a staircase of water falls some eight feet before rejoining the river below Kegworth deep lock. After crossing a stile and small footbridge the river side path curves 180 degrees to the left and rejoins the original path where the walk commenced at Kegworth Bridge.

Points of Interest

Kegworth is one of those places that seems to fall between two stools in terms of its status. On the one hand it is too large to be known as a village but on the other too small to be a town. The history of Kegworth is most interesting and during the early part of the nineteenth century this manufacturing village was full of framework knitting workshops. At this time Kegworth was an expanding county town and even had a brewery with four malt houses. The church of St Andrew has a commanding view over the Soar Valley and is the focal point of the village. The tower is early thirteenth century although the remainder of the church is fourteenth century. The Anchor Inn at Kegworth Bridge or the Ye Olde Flying Horse in the village both have a superb range of beers and choice food and refreshments are recommended at both.

Sutton Fields House, near Sutton Bonington was built in the late 1860s and is a fine example of later Victorian workmanship. Originally constructed for Mr Tidmas, an eminent surgeon from Manchester, who came to this area to become a lace manufacturer after marrying a woman from Nottingham. The house had little impact on the village as there was already a Manor House and a Hall in Sutton Bonington. It was always looked upon as the third house on the list for giving donations. A typical example would be where the Manor and the Hall would give a donation of £500 to the church, while Sutton Fields House would give £250.

The School of Agriculture (its proper title is the Sutton Bonington Campus of the University of Nottingham) has about 372 undergraduates and 120 post-graduate students studying for degrees in agriculture, various agriculture sciences and food sciences. The faculty has world wide reputation for research. In 1935 the college purchased a large Victorian house called The Elms which is now used by the Veterinary Investigation Centre of the Ministry of Agricultural, Fisheries and Food. During the First World War the school was used as a prisoner of war camp for German officers; a Captain von Müller led an escape of 22 prisoners by means of an underground tunnel. All but one of the prisoners were re-captured.

Footnote

An ideal walk for all the family either as an evening stroll during the summer months or a short winters walk to blow away the cobwebs. The footpaths are easy to follow and the fields are teeming with wildlife. There is even a pub at the end of the walk to quench your thirst. For a longer walk an idea is to combine this walk and walk number 17 to Zouch, giving a round trip of eight miles.

Walk 19: Red Hill and the River Soar

Distance: 6½ miles

Maps: O.S. Landranger 129, Nottingham and Loughborough area; O.S. Pathfinder 833 (SK43/53); O.S. Pathfinder 853 (SK42/52)

Location: From the A6 road at Kegworth follow signs for Kingston on Soar. Do not turn right to Kingston, but carry on to Ratcliffe on Soar village and turn right just before the church to Red Hill Marina. The road is clearly signposted to the marina and the walk starts from Red Hill Lock. Grid reference 492305.

Parking: Plenty of parking available at the marina.

Refreshments: The Captain's Table, Red Hill Marina (light refreshments only).

Public Transport:

By Rail: Nearest British Rail station is at Loughborough

By Bus: No bus service to Red Hill Marina. However, the walk could start at the cross-roads in Kegworth village. A frequent Leicester/Loughborough/Derby service operated by Kinch Bus and Barton Bus call at the village.

In the shadow of Ratcliffe Power Station lies the busy Red Hill marina clustered around Red Hill Lock on the River Soar. A popular haunt for both fisherman and boaters the river and marina is dominated by the closed proximity of the eight cooling towers of the power station. The classic walk follows the River Soar to Kegworth then returns over fields to the River Trent and the Derbyshire border at Trent Lock. An interesting riverside footpath then passes the junction of Rivers Trent and Soar and the magnificent railway bridge structure that takes the Midland Mainline Railway into Red Hill Tunnel.

The lock-keeper's cottage at Red Hill lock.

The Route

Cross over Red Hill Lock Bridge, number 57, which is the last lock between the River Soar and River Trent and is only three feet in depth. Turn left onto the riverside path opposite The Captain's Table café. Go over a long wooden footbridge then pass through a gate to join the River Soar footpath, leaving behind the many boats moored at the marina.

Climb two stiles in quick succession and from here there is a really striking view of Ratcliffe Power Station and railway line that feeds coal trains into the complex. The river sweeps round to the left and after crossing two more stiles and a footbridge, Ratcliffe Lock will be reached. The new lock of Ratcliffe is considerably deeper than the old lock which is noted alongside and is closed to river traffic.

Continue ahead now walking along Ratcliffe Cut keeping a sharp eye out for kingfishers, as this stretch of quiet water is renown for sightings of this small pretty bird. Go beneath the A453 road bridge, where to the left is a weir and behind that the church spire of Ratcliffe on Soar.

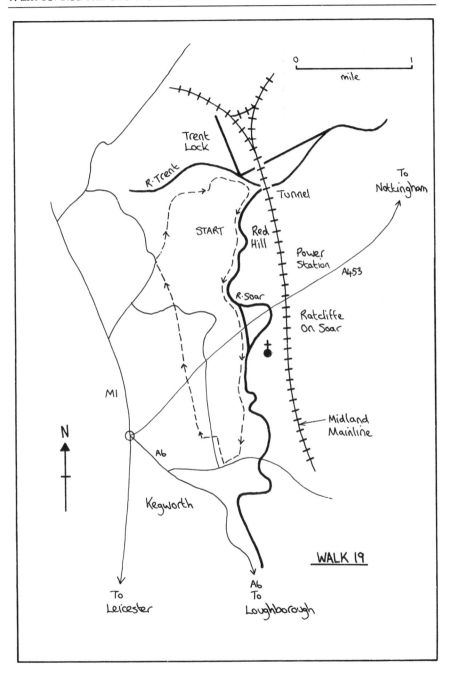

A little further ahead turn right over a footbridge and left to join the raised flood bank to a stile. Continue ahead along the flood bank, which gives a fine view of the River Soar below, climbing several stiles as you progress. Pass a farm metal gate on your left to join a field path and from here the river meanders away to your left.

Keeping a hedge to your left, follow the field perimeter footpath towards the spire of Kegworth church and pass through a gate. The well-used field path crosses two fields and brings you to an alleyway and the road. Turn right along Station Road heading towards Kegworth village as far as the cross-roads and turn right onto Long Lane noting a Midshires Way footpath sign. Walk along this road for 300 yards to a public footpath sign on the left adjacent to a new Severn Trent Water treatment plant.

Follow the obvious path ahead to the end of the field, then turn right through a gap in the hedge and cross a small paddock to a fence type stile. Cross the next field in the direction of the arrow to a hedge gap, then go over two more fields to a public footpath sign by the A453 road. Cross the busy road to a public footpath sign where an obvious field path now leads away from the road. Go beneath two sets of electricity transmission lines and to the right once again Ratcliffe Power Station dominates the scene.

Turn right, then left over a stream and keeping a hedge to your left follow the field perimeter hedge to a grassy track and the road. Cross to a Midshires Way footpath sign opposite where an obvious field footpath runs alongside the telephone poles and wires to a yellow topped marker post and a gate. Cross a stream, then go through another wooden gate where a field footpath brings you to a road.

Immediately turn right through a gate onto a wide grassy field track and follow the track ahead. In due course turn right and then left still following the field perimeter hedge. It appears that the footpath has been diverted here and instead of crossing the field you have to walk around the perimeter field edge. Over to your left is the village of Sawley, Derbyshire and the magnificent railway viaduct that takes freight trains over the River Trent.

At an electricity pylon turn left and, keeping a wood and then a lake to your right, continue along the field-edge path to a wooden gate. Once over the stream, turn right where a track leads to a gate and continues on then through the next field. Beware this field may contain a bull especially if there are calves in the vicinity but luckily the field is not too long to cross to the next gate. Walk around the next field to the left then cross a pasture field keeping a stream close to your right. There is not a definite path here to follow to reach the River Trent.

Turn right onto the raised grassy flood bank and pass the sailing club using the stile provided. Across the River Trent is a magnificent view of Trent Lock, where a colourful scene of boats, sailing boats, fishermen, two pubs and the Erewash Canal all impinge on each others business but makes a spectacular sight to the observer. A little further along the raised flood bank path the junction of the Rivers Trent and Soar is encountered. Here a magnificent steel bridge spans the River Trent that takes the Midland Main Line Railway over the water and into Red Hill Tunnel. The tunnel was built in 1838-1839 with ornamental portals and remains little unchanged since it was constructed by the Midland Counties Railway.

Follow the path around to the right, now following the River Soar and skirting to the left of Red Hill. An interesting fact here: it is known that during the days when horses were used for towing boats, at the junction of the River Trent and Soar there was no bridge and horses had to be carried across the water by ferry to the north bank of the River Trent while the barge was pulled across by ropes. The riverside path passes many chalets with well-kept lawns to the water's edge and then the picturesque Lock Keeper's Cottage. To return to the lock you need to continue on the riverside path over a footbridge to a stile then retrace your steps over the long wooden footbridge to the lock at the marina.

Points of Interest

Ratcliffe on Soar is a very small but exceptionally pretty village in the neighbouring county of Nottinghamshire. The notably feature of the village is the church and its spire. A landmark that can be seen from many miles around. Built in the thirteenth century the church has unusual white washed walls and many stone effigies mostly dedicated to the Sacheverell family.

Ratcliffe on Soar Power Station was built in the 1960s on a 384 acre site close to the River Soar and River Trent, alongside the Midland Main Line Railway. Commissioned in 1970, the power station has eight cooling towers standing some 350 feet high and one chimney that is 650 feet tall. Ratcliffe burns six million tonnes of coal each year with the majority of the coal being brought in by rail from the Nottinghamshire coal fields. It has a stock pile of coal in the region of 1.5 million tonnes. When working at full capacity Ratcliffe can produce sufficient electricity to satisfy the needs of two million people approximately. Owned by Power Gen the biggest customer that the power station has is East Midlands Electricity, and is one of the most efficient power stations in the country.

Footnote

The walk will appeal to the transport minded walker with waterways, railways, tunnels, bridges and cooling towers being at the forefront. East Midlands Airport at Castle Donington is close by and planes are often seen overhead. If you are not interested in transportation have no fear, as there are plenty of other beautiful countryside scenes to muse over and enjoy in this underrated part of north-west Leicestershire.

Walk 20: Cropston and its reservoir

Distance: 6½ miles

Maps: O.S. Landranger 129, Nottingham and Loughborough area; O.S. Pathfinder 874 (SK41/51)

Location: The furthest point of Cropston Reservoir is six miles north of Leicester on the B5330 Shepshed to Rothley road. The walk starts at the entrance to Bradgate Park at Hall Gates, Cropston. Grid reference 542114.

Parking: Hallgates car park, Bradgate Park, Cropston. Honesty box 50p.

Refreshments: Reservoir Inn, Cropston

Public Transport:

By Rail: Nearest British Rail station is at Leicester

By Bus: Leicester/Loughborough service operated by Barton Buses or Midland Fox.

An exhilarating walk for the discerning walker that encapsulates Leicestershire's best known and much loved Bradgate Park, Victorian Cropston Reservoir, and Swithland Woods right in the heart of the Charnwood Forest. Although the Reservoir is private with no public access, two superb footpaths and bridleways follow around close to the water's edge and from these rights of way the views are astounding and reminiscent of the lowlands of Scotland. The mug shaped Old John Folly stands proud overseeing the activities within Bradgate Park and is visible for the majority of the walk

The Route

The peaceful rolling hills of Bradgate Park have become so popular over the last decade that the Country Park now figures in the top ten visitors attractions for this Country. At weekends crowds flock to the Country Park (there are three entrances in all) and it is prudent to arrive at Hallgates car park as early as possible. Do not get alarmed as this beauty spot is more than able to cope with its increased popularity and the Bradgate Park Trust rangers are always on hand to control the flow of visitors.

Enter Bradgate Park via the wooden kissing gate where a tarmac path is joined. The path runs the length of the Park to the entrance at Newtown Linford and it is possible that on occasions vehicles may use the wide path. Almost immediately there is a fine view of Cropston Reservoir on the left and as progress is made through the Park the hills to the right begin to open out. Look out for red and fallow deer wandering free in the Park or hiding in the bracken. A recent addition to the Country Park is the acquisition of a Visitors Centre which is open every afternoon between 14.00 hours and 17.00 hours and is well worth visiting. There is a charge and full details are displayed on the information board outside.

Upon reaching the ruins of Bradgate House, and incidentally the ruins and chapel are open to view on Wednesday, Thursday, and Saturday afternoons during the summer, turn left over a small bridge that extends across the River Lin. Bear left onto a grassy path heading for a kissing gate on the extreme left, then skirt a wood to the left. Climb two stiles in quick succession and head for a yellow-topped

Cropston reservoir seen from Bradgate Park (Sandy Biggs)

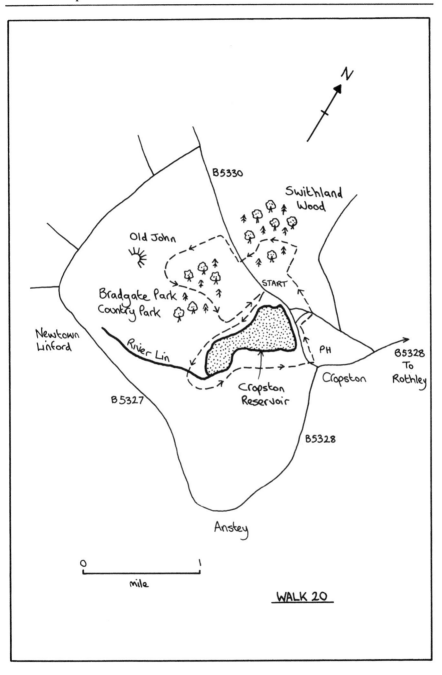

marker post where a field perimeter path is now taken. Cropston Reservoir has been rejoined but at this point the path will be difficult to follow especially during the summer as it becomes overgrown. Quickly the field path swings to the right and is much more easy to walk along. As you climb to a gate the views of the reservoir with a tiny boat-house and the rolling hills of Bradgate Park opposite are quite magnificent. It is unbelievable that the City of Leicester is only six miles away.

Turn right onto a well-used bridleway and a wide grassy field track runs parallel to the reservoir for about a mile to reach a gate. Continue along the lane into the pretty village of Cropston passing an old thatched cottage called Apple Tree Cottage on the right to a road junction. Turn left and opposite is the Reservoir Inn where refreshments may wish to be taken. The Inn previously was a Manor House and is a splendid white building set in beautiful surroundings. The B5330 road crosses the dam of the reservoir and from here is a view that surpasses all others of the Reservoir, Old John Folly, and Bradgate Park. At the road junction bear right and in 50 yards on the left is a public footpath sign.

Here a stile allows you to join a woodland path for a short distance before giving way to a field path. Walk past a pond to the left, then climb a stile into a small paddock. The path crosses two more paddocks before joining another footpath where you need to turn right for Swithland Woods. A secluded woodland path is followed which is a popular haunt for green woodpeckers as the tall trees give ideal security. At the end of the next field turn left along another footpath and enter Swithland Woods. The yellow flashes need to be followed through the woods as there are many other woodland paths running off the main arteries that lead really nowhere and it is easy to become embroiled in the woods for a serious length of time. Turn left past the deep lake, this former granite quarry is fenced off as it is very dangerous to go close to the edge, and follow the woodland path over a stream to the B5330 road and turn right.

Walk past the City of Leicester Waterworks Building built in 1920 and Filter Station to reach in 100 yards a footpath sign for Old John. A long track climbs slowly, and there is a fine view of the Folly to your right. Climb a stile then pass through a kissing gate into Bradgate Park and go to the right of Sliding Stone Enclosure. At an obvious meeting place of paths, bear left and head for Dale Spinney to your right. Keep the boundary wall of the wood to your right then turn right and cross to the next wood known as Coppice Plantation. Follow round then join a ridge path over the rocky outcrops that give a panoramic view of Cropston Reservoir below. Descend on the grassy path for ¼ mile to the kissing gate at Hallgates car park and the curtailment of the walk.

Points of Interest

Cropston Reservoir and Pumping Station were built in 1866 by Irish navvies, flooding about 200 acres of land. Water feeds into Cropston Reservoir from nearby Swithland Reservoir and is then treated. It is blended with other water from Derbyshire and eventually distributed across parts of Leicestershire.

Cropston is a hamlet of about 400 inhabitants in the parish of Thurcaston. It is tranquil with two fine pubs and at the cross-roads is a picture postcard thatched cottage that rivals anything of its type in Leicestershire.

Swithland Woods is part of Charnwood Forest with access rights existing to this large wood. It is a mecca for plants, moths, butterflies and birds.

Bradgate Park in total extends to 1100 acres, 850 acres are open to the public to enjoy while 250 acres are leased to local farmers. Bradgate was originally a series of parks and with the arrival of the Normans a deer park enclosure was formed. By 1500 the park had been extended to its present size and after many owners through the centuries in 1928 Charles Benion of Thurnby generously gave the park to the citizens of Leicester. The park is now administered by the Bradgate Park Trust with rangers being responsible for all aspects of park life from looking after the deer to dry stone walling.

Bradgate House was built between 1490 and 1500 by the Grey family who owned the park at that time. The house was one of the earliest unfortified great houses in Leicestershire with Lady Jane Grey living there for most of her life. On the death of Edward VI in 1553, Lady Jane Grey was declared Queen of England by a group of nobles opposed to Mary Tudor. Her reign was only for nine days when she was deposed by Mary Queen of Scots, and shortly after, along with other relatives was beheaded.

Old John Folly, Bradgate Park is a familiar landmark which was originally a windmill. There is a story surrounding the origins of the tower that in 1786 a beacon was lit to celebrate the fifth Earl's son coming of age and the large pole used to support the fire burnt through and fell onto a head of a popular miller, fatally injuring him. Being such a popular person, the Earl arranged for a memorial tower to be built to remember him by. From the Folly and toposcope nearby, there is an excellent view of the Park.

Footnote

A day should be given over for this walk as there is so much to see and enjoy. The walk covers about half of Bradgate Park and can easily be extended to encompass more of the Park by walking through to Newtown Linford. A visit to this village is recommended as there are two tea shops, a garden centre, pub, shop, and probably the best ice cream in the county can be purchased from Eric's ice-cream kiosk.

Walk 21: Mount Saint Bernard Abbey and Blackbrook Reservoir

Distance: 5½ miles

Maps: O.S. Landranger 129, Nottingham and Loughborough; O.S. Pathfinder 874 (SK41/51)

Location: Mount Saint Bernard Abbey is three miles west of Loughborough and is approached from either the A512 Loughborough – Ashby de la Zouch road or B587 Whitwick – Copt Oak road, Follow signs for the Abbey from both roads. The walk starts at the Monastery entrance. Grid reference 458163.

Parking: The Monastery allows walkers to park in the car park and offerings should be put into the collecting box in the wall.

Refreshments: None on walk, but the Belfry Holiday Centre, provides teas and refreshments, to be found on Oaks Road, close to the Abbey.

Public Transport:

By Rail: Nearest British Rail Station is at Loughborough

By Bus: No public transport to Mount Saint Bernard Abbey, but the walk may be started in Whitwick village instead. Leicester/Coalville and Loughborough/Coalville services operated by Midland Fox run fairly regularly stopping at the market place.

Without doubt the most spectacular scenery in Leicestershire is to be found in the Charnwood area where rocky granite outcrops date back to pre-Cambrian times, about 700 million years ago. These are some of the oldest rocks found in this country and Europe. The walk is extremely varied and surprising with notably highlights that will be relished are Blackbrook Reservoir, Fenney Windmill, Peldar Top Quarry and the unique Monastery at Mount Saint Bernard Abbey. Many magnificent views unfold in front of your eyes and this walk can be enjoyed time and time again all year round.

The Route

The walk commences from the spacious car park in the shadow of Mount St Bernard Abbey and you are reminded that the gates close to the Monastery at 19.30 each evening. Follow the driveway back to the road and turn right to reach a public footpath sign on the left in about 100 yards. This right of way is not shown on Ordnance Survey map no 129 as it has been diverted from Drybrook Lodge Farm some 200 yards to the left.

Go through the wooden gate to join a woodland path enjoying the scenic views to the right of the rocky Charnwood countryside. The path descends slowly through the wood and extends for ¼ mile to reach a track. Climb the stile to follow a field perimeter footpath to the right to eventually reach a stile in the far corner of the field. Blackbrook Reservoir is now seen stretching out to the left and makes a very picturesque sight set beneath the rocky outcrop.

Climb the stile and keeping a boundary wall close to your left cross the small field to a stile and public footpath sign where access is gained to a farm track. Turn left then go through a gate onto the bridge of Blackbrook Reservoir. Pause here for a few minutes and study the contours of the reservoir, then watch the ducks and swans swimming and diving into the clear water. Continue along the track away from the reservoir and follow for ½ mile to reach the road and turn left.

Charley Road is a quiet country road with little traffic and is followed for ¾ mile passing one or two very pleasant cottages before reaching the beautiful Fenney Windmill residence. Continue for a further 100 yards, leave the road to join a lane just before the busy A512 road, and a stile will be located on the left. An obvious field path weaves it way ahead to a squeezer in a dry stone wall and a private road is now joined to the left that leads to the gardens of Blackbrook Reservoir.

There is a legal right of way along this private road, which is very popular with local walkers and rambling clubs. It affords spectacular views across the green rolling hills. Cross a bridge over a stream and leave the road by the gates where access to the reservoir gardens is private and head for a yellow topped marker post to the right. A woodland path now skirts to the right of the reservoir gardens, alongside a dry stone wall, and is undulating in places before reaching a wooden gate. Turn left onto a field perimeter path and

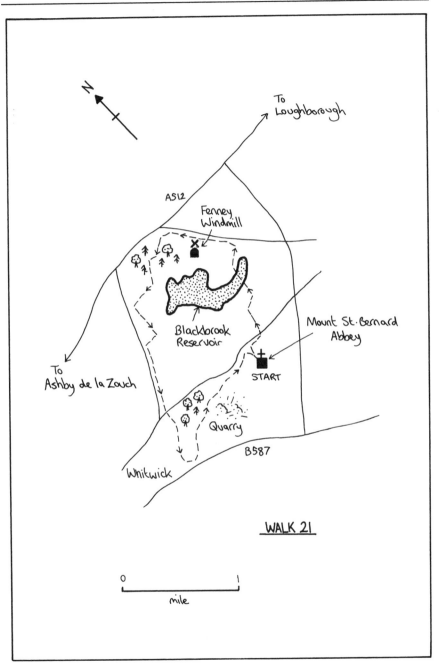

climb a hill to a marker post, then keeping a hedge to your right follow a long field perimeter path right round the field to a farm access lane.

Turn right along the access lane, noting that the lane past this point is private, to reach a busy road and turn left. Walk along this road, which climbs steadily for approximately one mile admiring to the left the rocky outcrop of High Sharpley. Regretfully, now there is no access to High Sharpley although many years ago a right of way did exist to this beauty spot. The local land owner managed to obtain permission to close off access to High Sharpley by stating that walkers were causing too much damage to his land.

At the cross roads turn left, and in 50 yards join a lane to the right and climb slowly to eventually reach a stile on the right. Pick up the obvious path to the left and then walk ahead noting a yellow topped waymark post to your left near to Vicarage Forest Farm. There are many unofficial paths in this area that have been made by local people out walking their dogs. Keeping a large hedge to your left descend a small hill to a stile and a short alley brings you to Hogarth Road. Cross to another alleyway and this will lead to Leicester Road in Whitwick.

Follow the B587 road to the left to a public footpath sign, then turn left along a wide track to join an obvious grassy path that is very well-walked. Soon the path twists and turns and passes through a wood. In places the path is narrow and rocky underfoot. To the left are more rocky outcrops and Rachet Hill is skirted to the right. If you stand on the grassy bank a fine view of Peldar Tor Quarry below will be enjoyed and it will leave you astonished that this large quarry is so unobtrusive. Continue ahead now downhill to reach a track where a right turn will lead you to a concrete stile on the left in about 50 yards.

Cross a number of short fields and stiles heading for the Abbey that is secluded in the trees ahead to a track. Go over the track and a short field path leads you to a stile and the road. Turn right along the road and at the bottom of the hill turn right at a public footpath sign where a path gives access to a wood. Follow the woodland path, then turn left over a unusual stile to join a grassy field path keeping a boundary wall to your right. A stile then leads you out onto the driveway of Mount St Bernard Abbey and you need to turn right to return to the car park.

Points of Interest

Mount Saint Bernard Abbey stands in 227 acres of prime Charnwood Forest land. Originally a monastery, it was built in 1835 and opened in 1837. In 1844 a permanent monastery was built, designed by the famous architect of the Gothic Revival, Augustus Welby Pugin on the site where it stands today. Four years later the Monastery became an Abbey and Dom Bernard Palmer was elected as its first abbot. Over 100 years after the foundation of the Monastery the Abbey church was completed but had to wait until the end of the Second World War for is consecration. There is a shop open six days a week between 14.30 and 17.00 and the Abbey church may be visited, except for Sundays, up until the closure of the Abbey at 19.30.

Blackbrook Reservoir was first constructed in 1796 to feed the Charnwood Forest canal but with the closure of the canal the reservoir was dismantled in 1804. However, between 1866 and 1882 the population of Loughborough grew by approximately 40% and Blackbrook Reservoir was re-constructed and completed in 1906. It is no longer part of Severn Trent water supply system.

Fenney windmill

Peldar Tor Quarry, Whitwick is thought to contain rock from one of the pre-Cambrian volcanoes that deposited volcanic material over Charnwood Forest. The quarry has long term reserves of hard rock that is mined and used as aggregate in the construction of roads. An agreement has been made with Leicestershire County Council not to spoil the environment of this lovely area.

Footnote

You are most welcome to look round the church of Mount St Bernard Abbey and park in the car park. Please respect the Cistercian Order of monks and only walk where you are allowed. Fenny Windmill is part of a private residence and there is no access to the beautiful restored windmill.

Walk 22: Thornton and its reservoir

Distance: 8 miles

Maps: O.S. Landranger 140, Leicester and Coventry area; O.S. Pathfinder 894 (SK40/50)

Location: Thornton village is located three miles south of Coalville and may be approached from the B585 Coalville-Desford Road or from the A50 road from Field Head. The starting point for the walk is the reservoir entrance opposite the Garden Centre. Grid reference 471074.

Parking: Roadside, either along Main Street, Thornton or by Reservoir entrance.

Refreshments: The Bulls Head, Thornton. Bulls Head Inn, Ratby.

Public Transport:

   By Rail: Nearest British Rail stations are Hinckley or Loughborough

   By Bus: Leicester/Ratby/Thornton/Coalville hourly service operated by Leicester Citybus – No Sunday service.

A gem of a walk that is quintessentially Leicestershire, visits the oldest and prettiest reservoir in the County. Now, no longer a working reservoir, Thornton's secluded setting is the ideal starting point for a magnificent day's walking. It is probably at its finest during autumn, when the rich colours of the surrounding woodland are very evident. The countryside around Ratby and Thornton is undulating with many good views to enjoy. The jewel in the crown is the large rocky outcrop of Markfield Hill that towers above the M1 motorway like a sleeping giant. You would be forgiven for thinking that you have stumbled into a fairy tale land.

The Route

Ignore the entrance into Thornton reservoir on Reservoir Road and walk along the causeway path with the reservoir to the left. From the roadside path are good views of the Victorian reservoir and as

Thornton church from across the reservoir

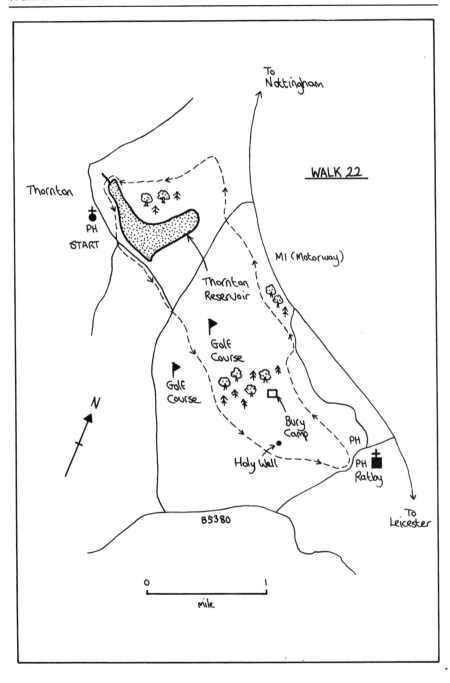

To Nottingham

WALK 22

Thornton

PH
START

MI (Motorway)

Thornton
Reservoir

Golf
Course

Golf
Course

N

Bury
Camp

Holy Well

PH

PH
Ratby

B5380

To
Leicester

0   1

mile

you climb the hill remember to look back for a superb view of Thornton village and church spire that protrudes into the sky.

At the road junction, cross to a public bridleway sign opposite, passing through a gate to join a track. Walk ahead on this extremely pleasant track, then turn right where a footpath bears to the left and continue ahead now passing through the playing area of Leicester Forest Golf Club. As this path is mainly enclosed by woodland in winter it is liable to be very muddy, but in places Leicestershire County Council have laid patches of granite stones to alleviate the problem.

Bear right through a wooden gate crossing the field in the direction of the waymark arrows keeping a dyke close to your right. A gate leads you into a wood and the obvious path is followed to an iron gate where a wooden fence is then kept to your right. Pass through the next gate then with a stream to your left descend a small hill to a track below by Holywell Farm. The farm gets its name from a holy well and it is said that the water is "anti-scorbutic" (prevents scurvy) and has never been known to freeze. In the fifteenth century, timber from nearby Burrough Spring Wood was used in the construction of Kirby Muxloe Castle. The track that you are now walking along was laid for the transporting of the timber.

In ¾ mile a gate is reached that leads you out onto a road, turn left and this road will eventually bring you to a road junction in Ratby village. Turn left along Main Street passing the Bulls Head Inn, a pleasant white-washed building, to Burroughs Road. Climb the hill passing another pub on the right, The Plough Inn. As you walk along the road look back over your shoulder for a different view of Ratby church. Ignore the first footpath sign on the right and continue for a further ¼ mile to the next public footpath sign on the right that points to the left.

A stile here gives access to a well-used field path that offers splendid views across undulating countryside. At the next stile a footpath picks up the line of a stream which is going to be your companion for the next ½ mile. At an obvious gap in the hedge enter a long straggling wood where the path is very narrow and at times difficult to follow to eventually reach a track.

Walk along the track to the right for a short distance, passing the beautiful farmhouse of Bondman Hays to the road and turn left with the busy M1 motorway a mere 100 yards now on your right. In about

100 yards turn left at a public footpath sign, climb the stile and follow the obvious field path ahead which is well-waymarked. At the horse stables walk along a track for 50 yards then cross a bridge keeping a wood to your right. As you walk alongside the wood, one or two caravans may be noticed hidden among the trees. These belong to members of the Charnwood Acres Country Club, which is a naturist club.

At the end of Whittington Rough a gap in the hedge gives access to a field path which is now followed for ¾ mile to Whittington Grange. Join the farm road and at the junction with the main road turn left to a public footpath sign on the right. From this track there are breathtaking views of Markfield Hill and village with the M1 motorway beneath cutting a swathe through the Charnwood countryside. In due course the track gives way to a field path which descends to a stream and after crossing the springy footbridge, ascend a hill to a marker post on the left and a Leicestershire Round footpath sign. Turn left and pass through a small wood to emerge out onto a field path where Thornton Reservoir will be viewed briefly to the left. The field path is now obvious to follow and crosses a number of fields before reaching a large wood where in front of you standing on a hill is the village of Thornton. Descend the hill on the field perimeter path adjacent to the wood climbing two stiles to reach the reservoir path. Turn right onto the accompanying path around the northern tip of the reservoir and follow the lakeside path towards Thornton church seen to the right. During the fishing season the pathway is closed from the church to the causeway and you will have to leave the reservoir at this point and return to the entrance by road through Thornton village. Out of the fishing season you may continue along the waterside path to the entrance passing an information board that reads "Please keep to the footpath, taking nothing but photographs, leave nothing but footprints, kill nothing but time" which is a lovely thought to carry with you on any walk.

Points of Interest

Thornton in the main is a long one street village with two pubs, several shops, a working men's club, and small post office. Situated on the edge of the fastly diminishing Leicestershire coalfield, the village looks down on the reservoir and has a fine church. The church of St Peter was built originally at the turn of the fourteenth century with the tower and spire rebuilt in the early sixteenth century. A massive south door believed to be fourteenth century is said to have come from nearby Ulverscroft Priory and the church is well worth a visit.

Thornton Reservoir is a prime example of a Victorian Reservoir, built in 1853, when water first flowed to Leicester to the Temperance Hall. The picturesque reservoir covers an area of 75 acres, but is no longer part of the Severn Trent water system as it too small and not cost effective. Thornton Reservoir is still owned by Severn Trent Water but is leased to Cambrian Fisheries who have professionally developed it into a boat and bank, brown and rainbow, fly only trout fishery. A good quality stone path encircles the Reservoir which is a permissive path. Out of the fishing season walkers are welcome to walk around the two mile perimeter and to enjoy the views that prevail. The path is not a public right of way and may be closed without notice at any time.

Ratby is four miles west of the City of Leicester and has historic connections with Roman and Saxon settlements. Bury Camp, about one mile west of the village, is an Iron Age Fort with a single entrance dating back to 100 BC. In Roman times it was probably a military camp formed for housing of workers who were building the Fosse Way at Highcross. There is no access to the ancient site. Old Hays Farm stands on a site dating back to the thirteenth century and a well-preserved moat has a footbridge across it that leads to the present farmhouse, built in 1733. Once again there is no access to the moat as the land around the farmhouse is private. Hays is a popular in this area and means "hedged enclosure".

Footnote

This walk passes through quite a number of woods and the paths are liable to be muddy even after lengthy dry spells. Make sure you wear walking boots or stout shoes as in places it can be hard going. Remember Thornton reservoir is now a fishery and only part of the perimeter path is open all year. Please respect this and also the reservoir car park as this is for the sole use of anglers between April and November.

Walk 23: Rearsby and The River Wreake

Distance: 3½ miles

Maps: O.S. Landranger 129, Nottingham and Loughborough area; O.S. Pathfinder 875 (SK61/71)

Location: Rearsby is an ancient village on the A607 Leicester-Melton Mowbray road about midway between both places. The walk starts at the post office on Brookside opposite the packhorse bridge. Grid reference 653145.

Parking: Alongside Brookside or Mill Lane in Rearsby.

Refreshments: Horse and Groom, Rearsby

Public Transport:

    By Rail: Nearest British Rail Station is at Syston

    By Bus: Leicester/Melton Mowbray service, fairly frequent, operated by Midland Fox.

This is a short walk that begins in the former Danish settlement of Rearsby in the Wreake Valley. The village is steeped in historic content with a magnificent seven-arch packhorse bridge across the pretty local brook. Alongside the bridge is a ford that cars have to use to reach the church and the north part of the village. Two old watermills on the River Wreake are passed which have both been lovingly and painstakingly restored to private residences but can only be viewed from the footpath or road.

The Route

Keeping the Post Office on your left walk along Brookside, then bear right onto Brook Street but do not cross the old packhorse bridge over Rearsby brook. The bridge is the show piece for the village and has stood there since 1714, having replaced an earlier wooden bridge. Tradition has it that six men completed the work in nine

The quaint seven-arch packhorse bridge across Rearsby Brook

days with a levy of 8d (eight old pence) in the £1 being put onto the
rates to cover the cost of the local tradesmen's work.

Continue along the road into Mill Lane where a Leicestershire
Round footpath sign to Rearsby Mill will guide you on the right. A
gravelled path leads around the bungalows, then a grassy path
brings you to a stile by a farm. Join the farm track ahead and follow
for nearly ½ mile to the gated level crossing. Take extreme care in
crossing the Leicester-Melton Mowbray busy railway line.

A pretty green lane leads away from the railway crossing and to
the left is the church spire of Ratcliffe on the Wreake in the distance.
The lane becomes a narrow path in due course, and maybe overgrown in summer, then after crossing a stream, a stile near to
Rearsby Mill will be met.

Before climbing the stile, read the notice and obey as this land is
private except for the footpath; you must not stray from the marked
route. A stile leads to a track by Rearsby Cottage which originally
was three tied cottages for the mill workers; it has now been
converted into a large residential small-holding. Turn left over the
River Wreake bridge and follow the track around the beautiful
exterior of Rearsby Mill to the millpond on the left.

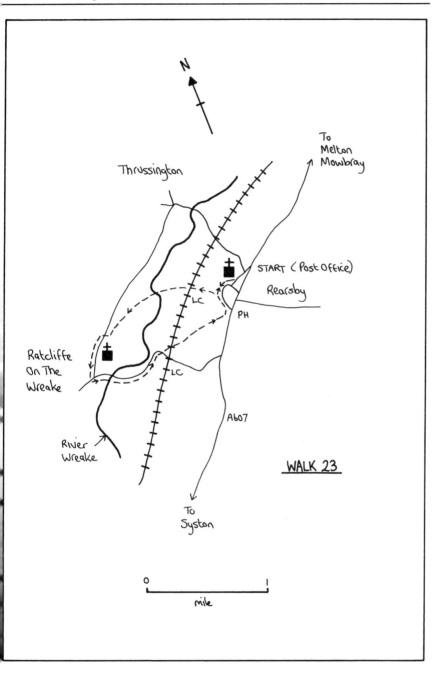

N

Thrussington

To
Melton
Mowbray

START (Post Office)

Rearsby

LC

PH

Ratcliffe
On The
Wreake

LC

A607

River
Wreake

WALK 23

To
Syston

0   1

mile

The present mill dates from 1835 and at that time flour was punted from the millpond along the River Wreake to both Rearsby and Ratcliffe villages. In the Domesday survey it was recorded that Rearsby had 2½ mills that were valued at two shillings. Towards the end of the 1940s the mill finally closed along with the bakehouse which produced the "Rearsby Loaf". However, the 100% wholemeal loaf is still made in Melton Mowbray and can be bought locally. Today the mill is a grade two listed building and contains much of the machinery including a water-wheel dated 1907 and two pairs of millstones, one pair from France being extremely rare. Please do not try to visit the mill as it is a private residence and privacy must be respected.

Leave the mill access drive by climbing a stile on the left where a path runs alongside the millpond to another stile. Cross a dyke by means of a plank, then after the next stile, climb a fence to your right and head in the direction of Ratcliffe on the Wreake church. Although there is no defined path to follow the way ahead is quite clear over the fields as either stiles or gaps in the hedge mark the route. Pass close to the high garden bank of several houses to an obscure stile in the field corner that is in much need of repair. Bear diagonally right to a wooden gate and poor stile by a farm, where the short farm track is taken to the road and turn left.

Walk along Main Street into Ratcliffe on the Wreake village following the road gradually up hill passing St Botolph's church on the left ignoring a public footpath sign on either side of the road. After ¼ mile turn left at the road junction onto Broome Lane heading towards East Goscote and follow the road down hill enjoying the spasmodic views of the Wreake valley countryside.

On the left is Ratcliffe on the Wreake Watermill, which had a Domesday Book value of three shillings, but ceased as a working mill in the late 1950s. At the time it was believed that this was the last watermill in Leicestershire to grind flour using only a wheel for power. The mill has undergone considerable refurbishment and a modern plaque states that the building is circa 1816. Once again this is a private residence which you are not allowed to visit.

Continue along the road going over the river bridge and after ¼ mile the road runs parallel to the river where there is high grassy bank to walk along. From here are good views especially of the village and the mill. Rejoin the road for a further ¼ mile to reach a public sign post on the left, which was badly broken at the time of writing some 25 yards from the road sign of East Goscote.

Climb the wooden fence next to the gate and cross the field to the stile that leads you onto the Leicester-Melton Mowbray railway. If all clear cross to the stile on the other side about 25 yards along the railway track. Cross the field to the hedge ahead, then turn left onto a well-used path to a stile. Bear right to pass beneath the electricity transmission lines to a farm gate and stile, which more than likely will be muddy. To the left is Rearsby House Farm and although it is a beautiful building the colour of the brickwork is rather insipid. Pass to the left of an old oak tree along a vague field path that in due course becomes much more defined before reaching a road.

Turn left along the A607 Melton Road and shortly on the right the Horse and Groom public house will be passed at the start of Rearsby village. Turn left in 200 yards onto Mill Road passing a pleasant half-timbered cottage called Olde House that was built in 1613 and follow the road through the village to return to the Post Office.

Points of Interest

Rearsby Village is a combination of old and new houses full of surprises around every corner. With a population of 883, the best part of the community is alongside the pretty brook overlooked by the church of St Michael. Built during the thirteenth century, it is a typical small parish church, the font being an unusual drum shape with four triple shafts attached.

Ratcliffe on the Wreake is a much smaller village of 135 inhabitants with several interesting buildings including the fourteenth-century church of St Botolph. Ratcliffe college was the first Roman Catholic college to be founded in England since the Reformation and contains an attractive chapel built in 1875 while the college itself was started in 1843.

East Goscote is a recently developed village built on the site of an M.O.D. establishment. Since 1976 the population of the village has grown quickly with much house building still taking place.

Footnote

A word of warning – do not attempt this walk after heavy and prolonged rain as the River Wreake floods easily especially around Ratcliffe on the Wreake and the road to East Goscote is often flooded and impassable.

Walk 24: Hoby and the River Wreake

Distance: 3¼ miles

Maps: O.S. Landranger 129, Nottingham and Loughborough; O.S. Pathfinder 875 (SK61/71)

Location: The village of Hoby is six miles west of Melton Mowbray located off the A607 Melton Mowbray – Leicester road in the Wreake Valley. The walk starts at All Saints Church on Main Street. Grid reference 669174.

Parking: Street parking only around the church. The village is normally quiet at all times.

Refreshments: The Bluebell Inn, Hoby – recommended for meals and bar snacks.

Public Transport:

By Rail: Nearest British Rail station is at Melton Mowbray.

By Bus: Melton Mowbray/Seagrave/Syston/Leicester service operated by Melton Bus and Coach – no Sunday service.

This all-year-round ramble that is full of surprises around every corner. Linger and discover the three Wreake villages of Hoby, Brooksby, and Rotherby each with their own unique history situated on either side of the Wreake Valley above the River Wreake. Throughout the walk there are marvellous views of pastoral countryside with a refreshing stroll by the water's edge. The Blue Bell, a Seventeenth-century thatched pub, at Hoby, just 100 yards from the church is well worth visiting and walkers are most welcome. Many places in the Wreake Valley are suffixed by the word "By" which reflects the Saxon and Dane law of the eighth and ninth century, when these civilisations came about.

The Route

Keep the church to the right as you walk through the village of Hoby to a road junction and turn left towards Brooksby and Melton Mowbray ignoring two Leicestershire Round footpath signs to the left. Walk along the road for a further ¼ mile to reach a second set of Leicestershire Round footpath signs and turn right over a stile to join a field footpath to Rearsby. At the next stile, bear left and keep a hedge close to your left to reach a market post. The footpath is now very obvious to follow over the next two fields and a stile emits you out onto a road.

At Lodge Farm opposite follow the farm road to the farmhouse then bear right past the house and head over two more fields to the bridge over the River Wreake. Cross the bridge, gated at both ends, bear left to a difficult ladder stile and cross the next field to the Leicester-Peterborough railway line. Take care in crossing the line, as it is not a boarded crossing, to enter the grounds of Brooksby Hall and turn left to a white gate and the road.

As you walk along the road to the right there are fine views of the church spire at Hoby back to your left, the church tower of Rotherby secluded in the trees to the left, and Brooksby church and spire to the right. At an entrance to Brooksby Hall turn left along a gated

The ironstone church at Rotherby, overlooking the Wreake Valley

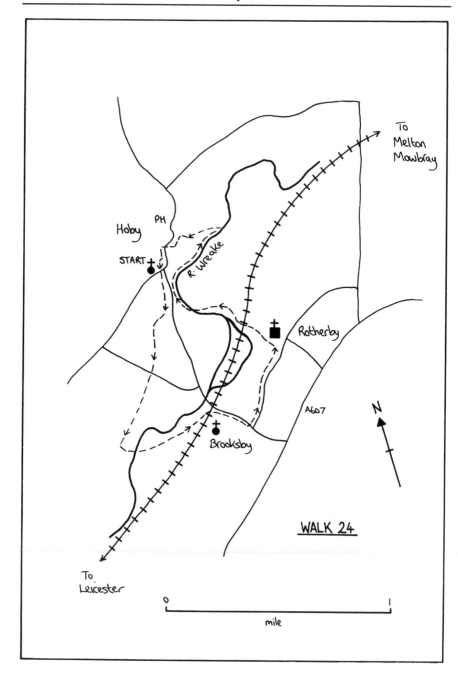

To Melton Mowbray

Hoby

PH

START

R. Wreake

Rotherby

A607

N

Brooksby

To Leicester

0   1

mile

WALK 24

road for ½ mile to Rotherby. Follow the road into the village, which won the best kept village in Leicestershire for two years running in 1965 and 1966 to the pretty church.

Turn left through a gate adjacent to the church where a obvious field path leads to the Leicester-Peterborough railway line again. Once more take care when crossing the line and a path now hugs the contours of the River Wreake. Time seems to have stood still in this part of rural Leicestershire and there are wonderful views up and down the Wreake Valley to saviour. Go over the farm bridge, turn right and pass through a gate alongside the Waterhouse. This pretty cottage was built in 1740 and used to be the offices for the water board when the river was canalised. Over 200 years ago this was a turning area for barges, and part of the canal can still be seen in the beautiful garden, now restored as a pond.

Follow the riverside path ahead, crossing the plank over a stream, below the hill that Hoby stands on to reach a marker post by the old mill bridge. Do not cross, but turn back towards Hoby to a stile and ascend a path to a track. Turn left along Back Lane to emerge out into the village opposite the church and the completion of a short but most enjoyable ramble.

Points of Interest

Hoby is a peaceful village built on a hill overlooking the Wreake Valley. There are many thatched cottages and timber framed buildings where during the early nineteenth century framework-knitting brought a source of income to the villagers. All Saints Church was constructed of mostly ironstone giving a sandy coloured appearance and in the south aisle there is a medieval stone altar. The best view of the Wreake Valley can be found from the beer garden of the Blue Bell and after a visit to this thatched pub it is not hard to see why callers travel many miles to enjoy a drink in such a serene setting.

Brooksby became a Danish settlement around 850 AD and virtually disappeared in the late fourteenth century due to the Black Death. Since then the parish has consisted of Brooksby Hall and church, built around 1220. The Hall was the home of the Villiers family until 1712. After the Villiers, the estate passed through the hands of several notable families including most recently Earl Beatty of Brooksby and the North Sea. Nowadays, the Hall is the Leicestershire centre for education and training in land based employment. Over 300 full time students attend the horticultural college learning a variety of countryside and farming skills. On the first Sunday in June each year a very popular open day is held for the public to view the Hall and the college activities.

Rotherby derived its name from a red-haired Dane 'Hrandi's by' and is one of the best kept villages in Leicestershire. There is no pub in the village but the fine church of All Saints with its perpendicular tower is well worth a visit. A recent business to come to the village is the wholesale nurseries and the many greenhouses can be seen from the valley below. At the wildlife garden there is a picnic table and seat where you may stop for a while and observe the natural pond and all its occupants.

Footnote

The footpath from All Saints church, Rotherby to Hoby passes through bucolic countryside. The view from the bridge over the River Wreake between the two villages accentuates the position of the twin settlements above the Wreake Valley. All paths are way-marked and easy to follow but beware if attempting this walk after very heavy rain as the Wreake Valley is liable to be extremely soft underfoot.

Walk 25: Asfordby and the River Wreake

Distance: 5 miles

Maps: O.S. Landranger 129, Nottingham and Loughborough area; O.S. Pathfinder 875 (SK61/71)

Location: Asfordby is three miles west of Melton Mowbray and can be reached by either the A6006 or A607 roads from Rempstone or Leicester respectively. The A6006 now by-passes Asfordby village, and the walk starts at the Village Cross on Main Street, which was formerly the A6007 road. Grid reference 707191

Parking: Melton Borough Council car park, Bradgate Lane, Asfordby – Free

Refreshments: The Blue Bell, Asfordby and The Bell Inn, Frisby on the Wreake

Public Transport:

By Rail: Nearest British Rail station is at Melton Mowbray

By Bus: Leicester/Syston/Asfordby/Melton Mowbray regular service operated by Barton Bus.

At the eastern end of the Wreake Valley lie the villages of Asfordby, Kirby Bellars, and Frisby on the Wreake all clustered around the River Wreake. This walk, which is hardly known outside of the area, offers a taste of waterside walking at its scenic best. It is popular with local walkers and village residents alike. The former gravel pits of Asfordby have been developed into a large nature reserve, with associated ponds given over to fishing, and is an ideal haven for naturalists. A notable landmark is the church at Kirby Bellars, remarkable for its isolated position and striking in appearance. Those interested in church architecture will enjoy visiting this superb building.

The River Wreake, with Asfordby church in the distance

The Route

With the village cross to your right, walk along Main Street heading towards Asfordby Hill passing the Parish hall built in 1927 to reach a public footpath sign and stile on the right. An obvious field path now runs to the left which is well-waymarked with marker posts ahead showing the way. From here you gain the first view of the isolated Kirby Bellars church over to the right.

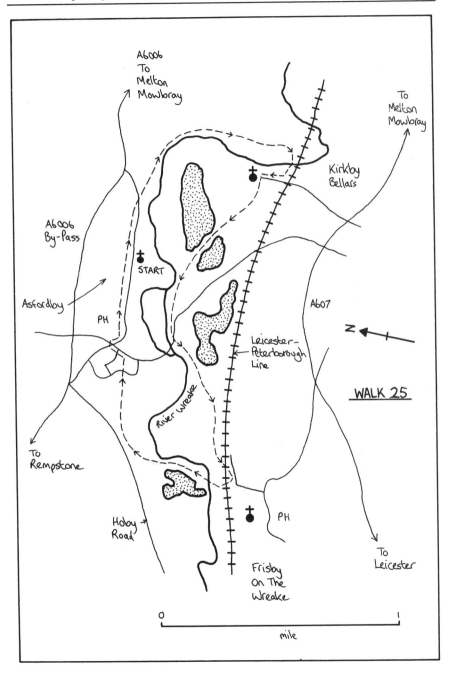

A6006
To
Melton
Mowbray

To
Melton
Mowbray

Kirkby
Bellars

A6006
By-Pass

START

Asfordby

PH

A607

Leicester–
Peterborough
Line

River Wreake

WALK 25

To
Rempstone

Hoby
Road

PH

To
Leicester

Frisby
On The
Wreake

0   1

mile

The footpath now joins the River Wreake by the old Holwell Works pumping house that took water from the river and pumped it to the works for cooling the blast furnaces; these were built around 1880 after the discovery of iron ore deposits in the Holwell Valley when the railway was laid. At its height the works employed 1500 men but now it has fallen to near 500. The blast furnaces are no longer there, and the works now produce cast iron manhole covers with water now being supplied from the works own reservoir.

The riverside footpath snakes alongside the water's edge and there are impressive views of the Wreake Valley with the church now much closer on the right. The river itself is alive with greenery, and marsh marigolds seem to flourish all the way along this part of the river. After ½ mile, opposite the church, the path darts away to the left over a field to a stile where you then bear right to a footbridge. Turn right over the old stone bridge that spans the river and walk along Washdyke Lane to a road junction by the railway bridge.

Turn right past Manor House and Manor Lodge to reach a public footpath sign on the right by St Peter Parish Church. A stile gives entry into a private nursery where a path must be taken to the right respecting that this is private land. At the end of a tree-lined avenue, climb a stile into a grassy field and bear left towards the lakes. From here, to the right, it is just possible to make out the box like buildings that cover the winding gear of Asfordby Mine.

A stile now gives you access to a path that intersects two lakes known as Priory Water, which until the early part of the 1980 was part of Asfordby Gravel Pits. This whole area is owned by Jelson Limited with Priory Water being leased to Leicestershire Wildfowlers' Association. The lakes have been developed into a nature reserve. Dogs must be kept on a lead and walkers must keep to the footpath as the actual nature reserve is for members only. Cross a stile to rejoin the River Wreake footpath and pass a pond to the right to a well-hidden stile in the field corner. Continue ahead and in due course you will emerge out onto a road by the river bridge.

Cross to a public footpath sign where a well-worn path leads back to the river while to the left is Kirby Lake, a popular expanse of water with local anglers. A stile to your right leads you onto a well-used field path and after going beneath the electricity transmission lines turn right. Walk alongside the Leicester-Peterborough railway line to a gated crossing. Take care when walking over the railway lines as modern Sprinter trains hurtle along the track at 70 mph. Join a farm track which brings you out just in the village of Frisby on the Wreake.

Depending upon the amount of time you have available you may like to walk up the hill into the village and explore or enjoy refreshments at the Bell Inn. Whatever you decide the walk continues from this point by turning right at Mill Deeping cottage and crossing back over the railway line to the River Wreake. Cross the bridge to join the pleasant path alongside the river passing to the right of another lake known locally as the Donkey Pit, while further to the left is Melton Mowbray sailing club where sailing craft can be seen tacking into the wind.

At a gate continue ahead, while the River Wreake moves away to the right. The fields around here in early August seem very popular with Canada Geese. Turn right along Hoby Road, then in 50 yards turn right at a public footpath sign where a path leads to the playing fields at Asfordby and enter the adjoining housing estate. Walk along Glendon Close, turn right and 100 yards proceed along an alley way to a road. Turn left then at the junction turn right onto Main Street and pass the Blue Bell pub on the left, then in about a further 100 yards the village cross will be reached.

Points of Interest

Asfordby has a number of charming old buildings found along Main Street and around the Parish Church of All Saints. The Saxon village cross, where the walk starts from, denotes a public meeting place and a track way halting point. The thirteenth-century ironstone church has an interesting nave roof with wooden supports that have angels holding musical instruments carved most decoratively. Recently, Asfordby has been placed on the map with the opening of British Coal's newest mine, located in the Holwell Valley. Design work for the colliery commenced in the middle of 1973 although it was not until 5th August 1984 that men appeared on site to sink the first shafts. The mine covers 80 hectares of ground and British Coal have been granted permission to mine under 60 square kilometres of land for mineral extract. It was originally planned that 1500 men would be employed but due to a lower demand for coal the total workforce is now only 500. Coal was extracted from the coal face for the first time in April 1995.

Kirby Bellars has a population of about 300 inhabitants and probably has a greater historic past than any other village in the Wreake Valley. Part of the village name is attributed to the Beler family who resided here and were related to the Mowbrays. Inside the church are two alabaster figures of Roger de Beler and his mother, circa 1360. The church of St Peter is unusually large and its isolated position would suggest that the original village disappeared, to be rebuilt centuries later to the south. In 1319 an Augustinian Priory was established to the north of the church but was dissolved in 1536. Later a Manor House now known as Kirby Park was built and in the early nineteenth century became the shooting box of St Francis Burdett, the Social Reformer and Fox Hunter. Nearby at Kirby Gate is where traditionally the first annual meet of the Quorn Hunt takes place. To the north and east of Kirby Gate deep furrows in the fields are detectable and this is believed to be the site of the original Kirby Manor House. The village has Roman connections with pottery being found in the churchyard of this period. The road that runs towards Stapleford Park and beyond is almost certainly of Roman origin.

Frisby on the Wreake is an attractive village with a stable population of just under 600. Situated on the south side of the River Wreake, Frisby was a linear village stretching along the main street, but has expanded over the years to become a thriving community. The old part of the village is to be found around the church, as was so many of the villages in this area. To the south of the village on the A607 are remains of an ancient Pilgrim Cross, known locally as Stump Cross, it marks a mid-point between Launde Abbey and Car Colston. The Bell Inn was originally three cottages dating back to 1759 before conversion into the pub and in the conservatory the back wall was part of the old village bakery.

Footnote

Please keep to the recognised footpaths on this walk. In two different place, Kirby Bellars nurseries and Priory Water, the path passes through private land with a right of way along the footpath. Do make the detour up the hill into the village of Frisby on the Wreake and explore the village. Refreshments are worth taking at the Bell Inn while the church of St Thomas a Becket should be viewed.

Walk 26: Manton and Rutland Water

Distance: 10 miles

Maps: O.S. Landranger 141, Kettering, Corby and surrounding area; O.S. Pathfinder 896 (SK80/90)

Location: Manton lies four miles to the south of Oakham, just off the A6003 Oakham-Kettering road, at the western end of Rutland Water. The walk starts from the Horse and Jockey public house, Manton – Grid reference 878047.

Parking: Roadside parking along St Mary's Road, Manton.

Refreshments: Horse and Jockey, Manton; Fox and Hounds, North Luffenham; Fishing Lodge restaurant, Rutland Water (Normanton entrance)

Public Transport:

By Rail: Nearest British Rail station is at Oakham.

By Bus: Oakham/Manton Crossroads/Uppingham/Corby Rutland Flyer Service operated by Midland Fox.

Enjoy a satisfying day's walking that takes in part of Rutland Water, the latest and most spectacular addition to beautiful Rutland. The massive reservoir was completed in 1977 and draws many thousands of visitors to its shores each year to partake in the many different activities on offer. This walk passes through villages and hamlets that have remained virtually unchanged for centuries, while the green and pleasant Rutland countryside is so utterly unspoilt, it is reminiscent of time gone by.

The Route

From the Horse and Jockey public house walk along St Mary's Road ensuring that the pub is on your left to the church and turn right onto Stocks Hill. A short way along this road on the left is The Forge, now a cottage; this was where the local blacksmith plied his trade. Built in 1582, many of the elder statesman of Manton still remember with affection the blacksmiths forge. The cottage still retains much of the original appearance and equipment inside. This is not the oldest building in Manton, that honour lies with the Priory Cottage which was built around 1350 and is to be found at the rear of the church.

At the road junction turn left onto Lyndon Road and very quickly the first sighting of Rutland Water will be made to the left. Above the reservoir is Burley on the Hill house, while in front is Lax Hill, and to the right is the beautiful Hambleton peninsula. Follow the road for ¾ mile, then after passing Rutland Nursery, turn left for Lyndon Hill Nature Reserve and cross the cattle grid to join a surfaced track. In ½ mile the visitors centre at the Nature Reserve will be reached, and for a reasonable admission charge maybe visited, but it is worth checking beforehand that it will be open.

Here, turn right joining the official Rutland Water footpath and cycle way, which is quite close to the water's edge. For the first mile the track passes through the Nature Reserve and ornithologists will particular enjoy this section of the walk as many species of birds dart from tree to tree all around. A cattle grid is crossed at the end of the Reserve and the track then begins to climb, revealing spectacular views of the reservoir.

The track undulates in places, keeping close to the water's edge and on the right is Rutland Water golf course. Pass through two woods in quick succession and after a sweeping right curve the sailing club and Edith Weston church is seen ahead. Go through an open gate and bear right, then follow the track around to the right to the sailing club and a metal gate. A surfaced road leads you past Rutland Sailing Club members building and in 200 yards turn left through a gate to rejoin the Reservoir track. In the distance is Normanton church museum which is well worth visiting although not passed on the walk. The track now leads to Normanton car park where there are a number of refreshment kiosks available as well as the Fishing Lodge restaurant that serves excellent food.

Turn right along Normanton Road to the crossroads in Edith Weston village where a road signpost points to North Luffenham opposite the RAF base. Walk along this road that passes alongside the old wartime aerodrome which is used for a number of training purposes but is no longer operational. Although Tornado planes are often seen over Rutland Water they are based at nearby RAF Cottes-

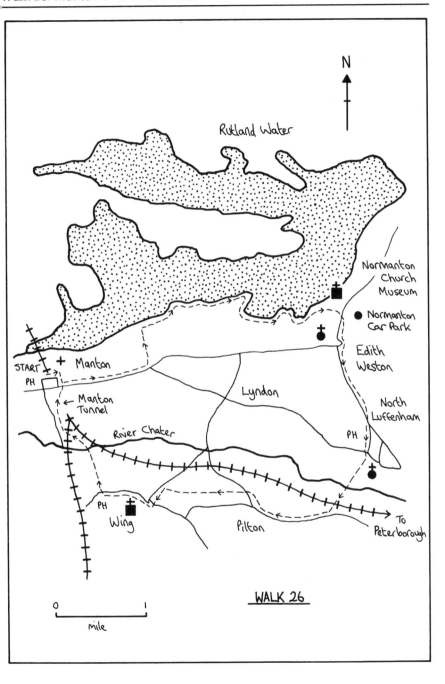

N

Rutland Water

Normanton
Church
Museum

Normanton
Car Park

Edith
Weston

START

Manton

PH

Manton
Tunnel

Lyndon

North
Luffenham

PH

River Chater

PH

Wing

Pilton

To
Peterborough

WALK 26

0   1

mile

more. Outside the entrance to the RAF base is a Bloodhound Mark One Surface to Air Missile and a Meteor fighter aircraft both on display and can be viewed from the road. After ¾ mile turn into Pinfold Lane and this leads into North Luffenham village. At the Fox and Hounds public house turn left onto Church Street to the Parish Church.

To the right of the church in the churchyard, is a stone stile and from here a field path descends to the River Chater and a bridge. Ascend the next field to a gate, then turn left along the road crossing over the railway bridge to a road junction and turn right to Pilton. Follow this quiet road for the next one mile to the crossroads, then turn right into the hamlet of Pilton bearing left past St Nicholas church to a public footpath sign to Wing on the left. A field perimeter path is very easy to follow and to the right is a splendid view of Lyndon Hall. Cross a track and continue ahead on a grassy field track over a number of undulating fields to the road. Turn left along the road to the junction, then turn right by Wing water treatment works and walk into Wing village passing the Parish Church. An interesting note is that the church clock was erected by the parishioners of Wing in memory of those from this parish that gave their lives in the Great War 1914-1918. Turn right opposite the Kings Arms, and at the corner, go through a gate by a public footpath sign onto a grassy vague path descending towards the railway line.

Cross over the River Chater bridge, bear left and head for the railway bridge by Manton Junction to a white wooden gate. Pass beneath the railway line to a public footpath sign on the right, and follow the enclosed path for ¼ mile next to the railway line. Above the junction signal box pass to the right of a house to join the access road and in 50 yards return to the enclosed footpath. At the top of the hill, Southview Close is reached, and at the road junction turn left, then right, back into Manton village to return to the starting point at the pub.

Points of Interest

Manton Village lies on top of the railway tunnel and in the late nineteenth century had its own station, but alas that is now long gone. St Mary's church is the main attraction of the village and dates from the thirteenth century. There are many fine houses and thatched cottages mainly built in the eighteenth century dotted about this pretty and charming country area.

Rutland Water spans some 3,100 acres and is the largest man-made lake in Western Europe being built in the 1970 to supply water to the developing towns of Northampton, Peterborough, Corby, Wellingborough, Daventry and Milton Keynes. The reservoir has a storage capacity of 27 thousand million gallons of water with the maximum depth of the reservoir being 110 feet. Many attractions have become established at Rutland Water at the four different entrances. Cycles can be hired by the hour or the day to explore the reservoir. In the summer a pleasure cruiser offers visitors the chance to see Rutland Water sailing from Whitwell car park.

Normanton Church is a famous landmark, encircled by water. It houses a museum showing the history of the reservoir. At night the church museum is floodlit, which is a most impressive sight. If you are still in the area after dark I suggest that you call back and savour the moment. It is open daily from April to October and Sundays in March, November and early December with a small admission charge.

Normanton Church Museum at Rutland Water

Wing Village has a maze with a difference! The turf maze has no hedges and nothing to stop you from cheating. Its origins are somewhat hazy but it is believed that the maze was used in medieval rituals with penitents having to crawl around the maze, blindfolded, on their hands and knees reciting prayers.

Footnote

There is so much to see and do on this walk that a full day must be allowed to ensure that all the interests especially of Rutland Water are seen. Several pubs on the route are passed which provide good refreshments while the Fishing Lodge at Normanton car park has an excellent restaurant and welcome to walkers.

Walk 27: Exton and its Lakes

Distance: 5 miles

Maps: O.S. Landranger 130, Grantham and surrounding area; O.S. Pathfinder 876 (SK81/91)

Location: Exton is situated one mile to the north of Rutland water and is approached from either the A606 Melton Mowbray-Oakham road via Burley or the A1(T) Great North Road going via Stretton and Greetham. The walk commences from the Fox and Hounds Inn, Exton. Grid reference 925113.

Parking: Limited parking around the green in Exton village.

Refreshments: Fox and Hounds Inn, Exton (Recommended)

Public Transport:

    By Rail: Nearest British Rail station is at Oakham

    By Bus: Melton Mowbray/Exton and Oakham/Exton service operated by Blands of Cottesmore. Note: There is only a return service on Tuesday and Wednesday respectively.

"Multum In Parvo" – so much in so little, is the Latin motto of Rutland and it truly describes this serene walk that begins at the picture-book village of Exton. Much of the walk is through the Exton estate and park, the home of the Earls of Gainsborough, which is extremely attractive especially around the lakes of the north brook. Overlooking the larger lake is a summer house known as Fort Henry, where, viewed from across the lake, the romantic castle puts you in mind of a fairy-tale adventure in the best Sleeping Beauty tradition.

The Route

Start with the seventeenth century Fox and Hounds Inn at your rear and walk along Stamford Road admiring several beautiful thatched cottages to reach a road junction. Opposite is a bridleway signpost where a short walk along New Field Road brings you to the entrance into Exton Park.

Go through the wooden gate adjacent to the cattle grid and join the estate road which is also the bridleway and pass through the next gate in a further 300 yards. There are yellow topped marker posts dotted periodically along the estate road marking the way ahead. The bridleway climbs and bears to the left where there are superb views of the park and Rutland countryside both to the left and to the right. In about a further ¾ mile a public bridleway and footpath junction is met and is marked by a modern and colourful signpost.

The Gothic Summerhouse of Fort Henry

Leave the estate road and join the grassy field track that carries on ahead and in places the track is undulating but extremely easy to follow. After ¾ mile the estate road is rejoined and from here the smaller lake of Exton Park is seen to the right. Follow the estate road between the two ornamental lakes then very suddenly the charming and pretty gothic summer house of Fort Henry is seen to the left secluded amongst the mature trees. The lake is a popular haunt for fisherman but access to the lake is only available from the public footpath that runs along the lake opposite the summer house.

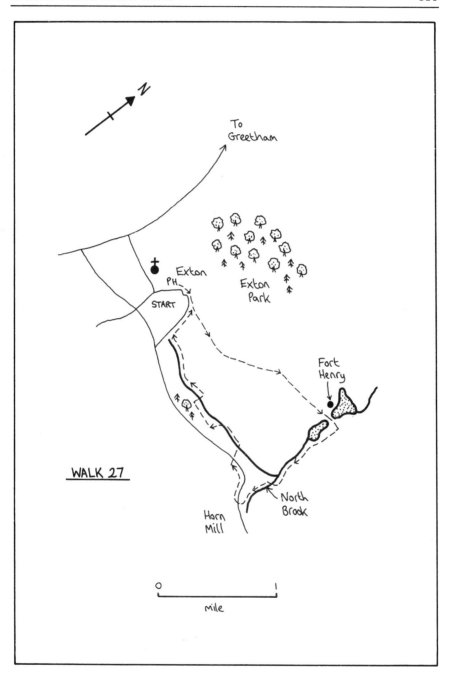

To
Greetham

Exton
Park

Exton

PH

START

Fort
Henry

WALK 27

North
Brook

Horn
Mill

0   1
mile

Turn right at a public footpath signpost and climb the stile, then walk ahead in the direction of the waymark arrow along a thin field path above the smaller lake. After climbing a stile join the estate road and then at the next public footpath signpost bear left along the thin field footpath keeping the stream to your right to a stile set in a boundary wall. Ignore the stile immediately to the left and do not cross the bridge over the stream as the path shown on the ordnance survey map has been diverted at this point.

Continue ahead keeping a fence close to your left and pass a pair of yellow waymark arrows on a wooden post, then ignore an old stile by the electricity transmission lines. A field track runs alongside the transmission lines for ¼ mile until switching to the left of the lines but there is no difficulty in following the well-waymarked route. Pass through a wooden gate, bear right to the stream and cross the bridge to the next stile. Turn left and follow a grassy track ahead passing above the trout farm at Horn Mill to a gate and a small fence by the road.

Turn right and walk along the wide grassy road verge to a footpath signpost on the right in ½ mile. Climb the stile and follow the field perimeter path, keeping a hedge to the right, to a hidden stile in the hedge. Descend to the stream below, cross the footbridge, then turn left alongside the stream. Again the footpath has been diverted from the map and follows the stream passing close to Cuckoo Farm on the left. Bear left at a waymark arrow to a stile, then cross back over the stream at the footbridge.

Follow a thin field path for ¼ mile to the next stile, then pass through a wood and cross over the stream again to join a thin field path. Continue ahead for ½ mile on the inclined path, which is waymarked, to a pair of stiles and at the next stile join a track to the left. Pass through a gate, and continue to the next gate about ¼ mile ahead to emerge onto a road.

Turn right along Empingham Road into Exton village, where the church will be glimpsed to the left, before reaching Exton estate and farm office building on the right. At the road junction turn left onto Stamford Road and retrace your footsteps to the Fox and Hound Inn.

Points of Interest

Exton Village is possibly the prettiest of all the villages in Rutland with many attractive houses and thatched cottages grouped around the shady green. The film *Little Lord Fauntleroy* was shot in the village and featured the church of St Peter and St Paul.

Exton Park dominates the village and once extended to 1500 acres of deer park. It is the home of the Earls of Gainsborough but the estate is now run by his son, Viscount Campden. The park is private and walkers are welcome but you must keep to the recognised footpaths and bridleways at all times. The church is within the park and contains a magnificent collection of nine monuments. For anyone interested in sculpture a visit to the church is recommended, although the key will have to be collected from the estate and farm office. The fourteenth-century church and spire was struck by lighting in 1843 and over the next 10 years was considerably re-built, but nevertheless is still one of the most appealing churches in Rutland.

Footnote

Many of the footpaths and bridleways, including the Viking Way, that pass through the park have been diverted or altered. I suggest before setting off on this or any other walk through the park that you purchase a map sheet for 10p from the Fox and Hounds Inn which shows all the rights of way around Exton.

Walk 28: Hose and the Grantham Canal

Distance: 6 miles

Maps: O.S. Landranger 129, Nottingham and Loughborough; O.S. Pathfinder 854 (SK62/72) and O.S. Pathfinder 834 (SK63/73)

Location: Hose is in the Vale of Belvoir eight miles north of Melton Mowbray. It is best approached from the A606 road via Long Clawson where the walk commences from the spreading chestnut tree at the green. Grid reference 736294

Parking: Around the green on the roadside. There is no official car park.

Refreshments: The Rose and Crown, Hose (Recommended). White Hart and Nags Head, Harby.

Public Transport:

> **By Rail:** Nearest British Rail station is at Melton Mowbray.
>
> **By Bus:** Melton Mowbray/Hose/Harby/Bingham fairly frequent 'Vale Runner' service operated by Barton Buses. No Sunday Service.

This walk closely follows the beautiful Grantham Canal which has an abundance of flora and fauna. It explores the two sleepy villages of Hose and Harby nestling in the attractive countryside of the Vale of Belvoir. Spend some quality time in each village examining the quaint old streets, the picturesque churches and the delightful public houses complete with hanging flower baskets. The village green with the spreading chestnut tree in Hose, so typifies this unspoilt area of Leicestershire.

The Route

From the large spreading horse chestnut tree at the junction with Church Walk and The Green follow around the green to the left keeping the children's play area to your right to a side road on the left. An alleyway at the end of the road leads you out onto the Long

Clawson-Harby road where opposite is the village hall. Turn right, follow the road around the playing fields to sign for a Mount Pleasant Farm and a no through road.

Go along this lane for 200 yards to a bridleway and public footpath sign by the entrance to the tennis courts. Join the grassy bridleway and make your way along the obvious track. Very quickly to the right there are good views of Harby Hills and woodland while to the left the last remaining houses in Hose village will be seen. After passing through two farm gates in quick succession the path now follows close to a hedge to your right and for the next one mile it is a really a case of crossing numerous short fields and passing through associated gates to reach a minor road.

Cross the road to an obvious track opposite which is bounded each side by a high hedge and walk ahead in the same direction noting to the right the pretty white farmhouse of Willow Farm. Take care as you negotiate the track as it is very rutted in places and a wrong step could result in a strained or twisted ankle. In due course the track narrows to a thin path and in a further ¼ mile it meets a farm track from the left. Turn left onto the wide track which eventually leads into Green Lane and on the right you pass a row of cottages knows as Rutland Terrace built around the turn of this century.

At Pilgrims Cottage, Harby, turn left along the road to Dickmans Lane on the right. As you wander along this lane there are many beautiful old cottages to admire, but none more so than Trevelyn's Cottage, built in 1610 which was originally a trio of cottages and later converted to one large desirable residence. Turn right onto Boyer's Orchard and follow for 100 yards to a wooden gate next to the Old Rectory. An alleyway leads into the church yard of St Mary and just past the church porch is a gate and a public footpath sign. Climb the stile, then bear left over this field to a white gate adjacent to the Grantham Canal and cross the concrete footbridge to the grassy tow path and turn left.

From the tow path there is a good view of the disused Langer Airfield that was home to Squadron 207 during the Second World War. This former RAF base, is now partially used by British Parachute Schools, for training and if you have the nerve you can make a parachute jump so long as sufficient sponsorship money is raised for charity. Further details may be obtained from the parachute

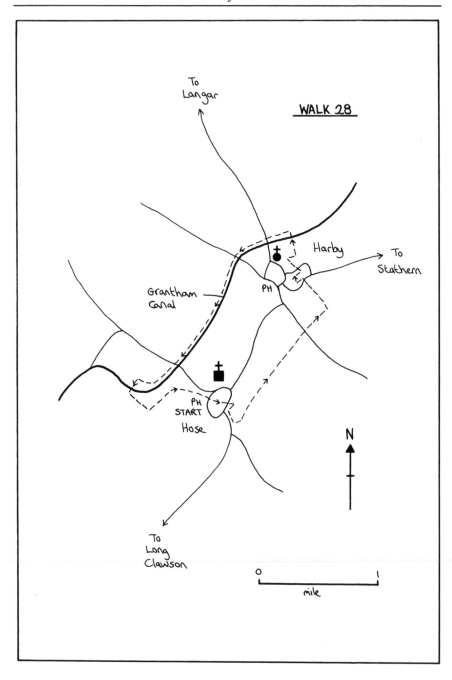

school at Langar. Cross Langar Lane where bridge 43 used to stand and pass British Waterways maintenance yard at Harby to rejoin the superb tow path enjoying the pleasant rural views. Next pass through the two gates either side of the Harby-Colston bridge and the tow path now passes the stump of an old windmill. The windmill was part of a large granary, which still stands, and the old wharf is also noticeable. It appears that the sails of the windmill along with the top storey were removed when Langar Airfield was developed.

The tow path sweeps majestically through the open countryside for the next one mile and surprisingly in one place the canal is extremely wide making it a popular haunt for swans, moorhens, and coots going about their business. Cross a farm track noting Hose church away to your left then go over the road at the side of Hose bridge. Along this next section of tow path you are likely to encounter sheep as the hedge that separates the path from the fields is rather sparse and sheep are able to push their way through to eat the lush green grass. In this instance there is truth in the old adage that the grass on the other side is greener.

Climb a gated stile, then in a ¼ mile leave the canal at Hose Lodge. A footpath encircles the farm to the right and although there is no obvious path, follow around close to a fence on your left. A farm gate gives access to a small field and you need to make for a gate alongside the canal now on the opposite bank. For the next 100 yards continue by the canal, then after crossing a stream turn right to follow the stream to a gate in the field corner. Pass through an untidy area of woodland for ¼ mile to reach a public bridleway sign and a track adjacent to Hose sewage pumping station. The track leads to a road junction in Hose village where a left turn will bring you to the Rose and Crown public house. This is a most interesting pub with a fine display of hanging baskets full of overflowing flowers. A board fixed to the brickwork of the building announces the real ales and their prices that the pub has on sale. Turn right into Middle Street to reach the green and the spreading horse chestnut tree.

Points of Interest

Hose is rather an unusual name for a village and upon investigation it appears that its name is taken from the Old English "homas" meaning "hills". To the south east of Hose are the Harby hills which the name refers. The compact village has a population of just under

The Rose and Crown at Hose

500 with about 150 dwellings of all ages having existed for about 2000 years. The church of St Michael that overlooks the village green is one of the best rural sights in this part of Leicestershire. Built in the fourteenth century the church is mostly ironstone and has been added to in the fifteenth century.

Harby Village lies nine miles north of Melton Mowbray on the edge of the Vale of Belvoir. Several houses date back to the early seventeenth century and are either timber or mud walled structures. St Mary church is medieval, built in the fourteenth century, of ironstone and much restored in 1870-1876. There are two excellent pubs in the village, situated opposite each other, and offer the walker a choice of pub food at good prices. The largest employer in Harby is Millway Foods Ltd on Colston Lane who are cheese manufactures. They primarily make Stilton cheese but as the consumption of this is seasonal (Christmas) other cheeses such as Red Leicester and Double Gloucester are also produced. Originally, the plant was opened in January 1976 by Unigate who then sold the site to St Ivel in 1988. Later, a management buy out took place and Millway Foods Ltd evolved. The milk for the cheese is collected everyday by milk tankers from the plant and mainly comes from farms between Harby and Melton Mowbray. The plant is not open to the public for visits.

Footnote

The footpaths and bridleways should present no problem as they appear to be fairly well-walked by local ramblers. However, there is a distinct lack of waymark posts and the only possible area where you could stray from the recognised path is from Hose Lodge back to Hose Village. Choose a really clear sunny day to get maximum enjoyment from this walk.

Walk 29: Plungar and the Grantham Canal

Distance: 8 miles

Maps: O.S. Landranger 129, Nottingham and Loughborough area; O.S. Pathfinder 834 (SK63/73)

Location: Plungar is located in the Vale of Belvoir just inside the county boundary with Nottinghamshire some 11 miles north of Melton Mowbray. The village can be approached by using the A606 or A52 roads from Melton Mowbray or Nottingham and is signposted accordingly. Start from the Belvoir Inn on Granby Lane, in Plungar. Grid reference 768340.

Parking: The Belvoir Inn car park, Plungar. (Kind permission of landlord)

Refreshments: The Belvoir Inn, Plungar. Tea rooms at Our Little Farm, Plungar. The Peacock Inn, Redmile.

Public Transport:

By Rail: Nearest British Rail station is at Bottesford

By Bus: Melton Mowbray/Plungar/Bottesford frequent service operated by Barton Buses. No Sunday service

---

Feast your eyes over the beautiful Vale of Belvoir countryside on a walk that begins in the chocolate box village of Plungar. The walk is always in the shadow of the fairy-tale Belvoir Castle and this far corner of Leicestershire has wonderful scenery which is so often overlooked by walkers. The grassy tow path of the Grantham Canal has a surprise awaiting you around every bend where it is possible to encounter a family of swans, goats and horses all enjoying the peace and quietness that this canal tow-path has to offer.

The Route

The Belvoir Inn is located at the crossroads of Granby Lane and Post Office Lane in the centre of the village. The pub was built around 1774 having originally been four terraced houses that at a later stage were converted into one dwelling, then about 100 years ago the pub evolved. Around the corner on Post Office Lane is the Old Post Office which is one of the oldest buildings in Plungar, built in 1764. A Royal Mail posting box is situated within the cottage wall.

Walk along Church Lane away from the Belvoir Inn, through the village to reach a footpath sign well-hidden on the left in a hedge. Unusually you now have to pass through an orchard to emerge out into a field and turn left. Cross to the hedge opposite where a field footpath leads towards the Grantham Canal. Turn right over a stile that is about 50 yards from the canal and follow the obvious field path ahead towards the church spire of Barkestone le Vale. Cross a line of stiles ahead, and in particular one stile is extremely narrow, and care needs to be exercised when climbing over it.

Turn right onto a lane by the canal bridge where 100 yards on the left a public footpath sign and stile will be located. As you walk along the field path superb views unfold to the left of the Vale of Belvoir while in the distance the first clear sighting of Belvoir Castle will be experienced. Turn right by a blue farm gate over a stile, where a field perimeter path now passes you close to the magnificent Barkestone le Vale village church. Ignore a footpath on your left unless you wish to visit the church and continue ahead to reach the road.

Turn left into the village, then turn right onto Chapel Street and follow around to the left to Town End. Turn left, then right at Rutland Square and in a matter of 100 yards a myriad of footpaths will be reached. Climb the recently new stile alongside a gate and head over the field again in the direction of a church, this time it is Redmile noting that Belvoir Castle is much closer to your right. Follow the line of repainted marker posts over a number of fields to eventually reach a stream alongside Redmile sewage plant. By an ash tree climb a double stile where the field path leads to a housing estate road in Redmile.

Church Lane is a quiet road that will bring you to Redmile church in the main part of the village. Turn left, and on the right is the Peacock Inn where the car park is the old canal wharf. The pub is in the Egon Ronay pubs and inns guide and makes an ideal halfway stopping off point, but look out for the table that is reserved for the locals only – sit there at your peril! Continue along Main Street for 50 yards to reach a gate just over the hump backed bridge of the Grantham Canal.

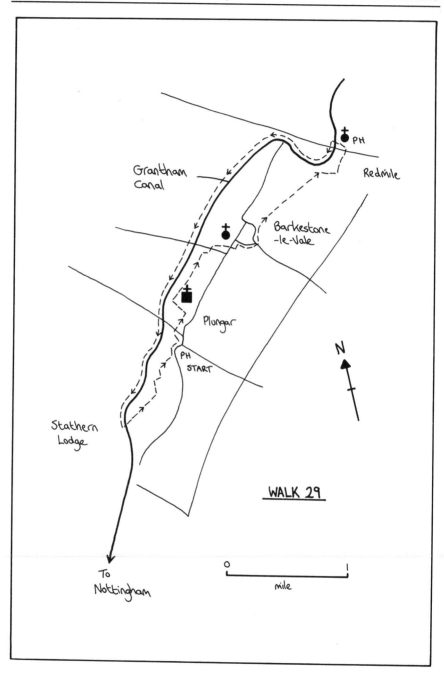

Grantham Canal

Redmile

Barkestone
-le-Vale

Plungar

PH
START

Stathern
Lodge

N

WALK 29

To
Nottingham

0 ─────────────── 1
        mile

Go beneath Redmile Town Bridge (No 54) and join the grassy tow path walking in the direction of Barkestone le Vale indicated on a British Waterways Plaque that states the village is two miles due west. Now comes an extremely pleasant walk along the grassy tow path with lovely views into the Vale of Belvoir countryside. The tow-path swings to the right and during the summer in places the vegetation is so high that it completely obscures the water in the canal. Cross Redmile Lane, at the site of Redmile Mill bridge, where there used to be a hump-backed bridge. Rejoin the grassy tow path heading in the same direction. On the right the visual remains of the Melton Mowbray-Bottesford/Newark railway branch line will be noted.

For the next one mile the tow path passes through a cutting and there is very little to see other than the canal life but this is not disappointing. Mallard ducks swim backwards and forwards across the canal, while moorhens weave and dive looking for food, swans glide gracefully by and this more than compensates for the lack of distance views. Bull Rushes grow in profusion along this section of canal and a hobby of local people is to pick the plant when it has flowered, lacquer them and place them in a vase along with other grasses as a flower arrangement which can last up to 12 months.

Go beneath bridge 51 and in a further ½ mile bridge 50 which may be recognised from the earlier part of the walk. In a matter of 200 yards a key shaped mile post will be passed indicating that at this point you are 21 miles from the Trent. It is likely that you may encounter a pair of goats on the tow path but do not worry they are quite friendly, as are the swans and family that stretch out on the grass by the water's edge during the summer sunshine. At the site of Plungar Bridge, cross the road and rejoin the tow path now heading for Stathern Bridge 1½ miles away.

What is so interesting about the disused Grantham Canal is the ever changing canal water and habitat. At times the canal seems choked with reeds while other times the water is exceptionally clear. Pass beneath the remains of the railway bridge 47a, then bridge 46 which is still in place. This bridge took the Melton Mowbray-Bingham branch line over the canal. In a further ¼ mile leave the canal at a concrete bridge at Stathern Lodge.

Pass through a gate, then follow the obvious field path away from the canal to cross over the old railway line. Keeping a hedge close

The towpath of the Grantham Canal between Plungar and Barkestone

to your right, walk along the wide grassy path and in the distance once again Belvoir Castle will be seen. In the late evening sunshine the castle almost comes to life and is very reminiscent of a fairy tale castle so often depicted in books and films.

A track leads over the second dismantled railway line in this area where a gate then gives access to a field path. In about 100 yards on the right is "Our Little Farm" at Lodge Farm where tea rooms are available from the walk for refreshments. Pass to the left of the farm, following the waymark arrows, then a field path leads to the road in Plungar. Walk along Harby Lane for ¼ mile passing the war memorial where seven men in the first world war and one man from the second world war lost their lives to Granby Lane. Turn left and in 100 yards on the left is the Belvoir Inn public house car park.

Points of Interest

Plungar is a large sleepy village close to the Grantham Canal with a pub and church. The dedication of the church is to St Helen, the patron saint of dyers, nailsmiths, needlemakers and wells, and its origin can be traced back to the eleventh century. It was restored and enlarged in 1856 by Reverend Burnaby, while in a tower two bells are still in use that were cast in 1747.

Our Little Farm, Lodge Farm, Plungar is passed on this walk and there is access into the tea rooms where home produced cold lunches and afternoon teas are available. For a small charge you can visit the traditional Victorian farmyard where rare and commercial farm animals are housed in nineteenth-century farm buildings and paddocks. The farm is open from late March to October 31st but closed on Mondays except for bank holidays.

Barkestone-le-Vale is a much smaller village than its neighbours of Plungar and Redmile and at one time supported three pubs. There is still one traditional pub in the village, along with a restored sixteenth-century church.

Redmile derives its name from the soil which has a high ironstone content and gives a red "mould" appearance. The village has a thriving community, but it is now nothing in comparison with former times. Redmile's most famous resident was Thomas Daffy, a parson, who resided there from 1666 to his death in 1680. As well as being a reputed preacher he also invented "daffy's elixir" which at the time would cure any aliment.

Belvoir Castle is close by and the home of the Duke and Duchess of Rutland. There are notable pictures in the state rooms, while the castle is also home for the 17/21st Lancers Museum. Many television programmes and films have used the castle as filming location for period dramas. The house is open to the public during most days from 1st April to 1st October but it is advisable to check first if a visit is contemplated.

Footnote

This is an easy flat walk through beautiful Vale of Belvoir countryside along well-waymarked footpaths which are a joy to tread. I found the wildlife fascinating along the canal tow path and although no narrow boats can use the Grantham Canal this did not detract from the enjoyment.

Walk 30: Bottesford and The Grantham Canal

Distance: 10 miles

Maps: O.S. Landranger 130, Grantham and Surrounding area; O.S. Pathfinder 835 (SK83/93)

Location: Bottesford is 16 miles north of Melton Mowbray and is by-passed by the busy A52 Nottingham-Boston road. The walk starts at the church of St Mary The Virgin by the entrance gates. Grid reference 806393.

Parking: Along Church Street, near to the Church

Refreshments: The Red Lion, The Bull Inn, and Rutland Arms, Bottesford.

Public Transport:

By Rail: Nearest British Rail station is at Bottesford

By Bus: Melton Mowbray/Stathern/Bottesford fairly frequent service operated by Barton Buses (Vale Runner No 2). No Sunday service.

Without doubt of all the Leicestershire honeypots, Bottesford is the least well-known possibly due to its most northerly location within the county. You will be seduced by the grandeur of the Vale of Belvoir countryside and the magnificent Belvoir Castle that overlooks the Grantham Canal. There is a chance to sample long distance walking along part of the Viking way but the *pièce de resistance* of the walk is Bottesford church with its spectacular spire and remarkable collection of tombs of the Lords of Belvoir.

The Route

Begin at the entrance gates to the church and walk along Church Street passing a number of fine old buildings including one dated 1761 to The Red Lion on Grantham Road and turn right. Follow the road around to the left by the Bull Inn, then turn left onto Belvoir Road opposite the Rutland Arms. Unbelievable there are three public houses within 200 yards of each other and they all offer good refreshments.

Turn left by a sign for the village hall and by the children's swings turn right onto a footpath to a stepping stile in the corner of the playing fields. Skirt round a large detached house to the right to a stile and follow a well-waymarked field path to the next stile. At this footpath junction bear left around the field perimeter to an obvious hedge gap and continue around the next field to the left to a stile alongside by busy A52 road.

Take extreme care in crossing this fast road to the stile and public footpath sign opposite where a diagonally left field path brings you to a gate. Turn right along the quiet road and follow for ¾ mile to the Grantham Canal enjoying the splendid site of Belvoir Castle ahead in the distance. At Easthorpe Bridge, turn left along the obvious grassy tow path heading for Muston which is 2½ miles to the east.

Walking along the picturesque grassy path there are many fine sites of ducks and geese swimming in the clear water and the opposite bank is an ideal haven for swans to nest and bring their young into this world. Cross a farm track at Muston Gorse Bridge and from here is probably the best view of Belvoir Castle to the right. Rejoin the grassy path by passing through the access gap next to a white gate and continue along the path in the same direction noting to the left the landmark of Muston church spire. The canal is quite wide for the next one mile to Longore Bridge and many pleasant rural views of the Vale of Belvoir landscape are available.

Go beneath the brick-built farm bridge number 58 (Longore Bridge) noting Muston village close to your left. Between this bridge and the next one, bridge 59 – Muston Road Bridge, the border into Lincolnshire is crossed. At this bridge, a small public footpath sign post shows the way along the canal. Bear right and pass the disused Muston Lock, now fenced off as the lock has been drained, and continue ahead now following a footpath instead of the permissive tow path for ¼ mile before crossing the River Devon.

In quick succession two more disused locks are passed, Stenwith and Kingstons, and like Muston Lock the gates and lock mechanism have been removed and a series of steps have been built to allow the water to fall to the lower level of the lock bottom. A further ¼ mile will bring you to Stenwith Bridge where the canal is left by climbing up to the road bridge.

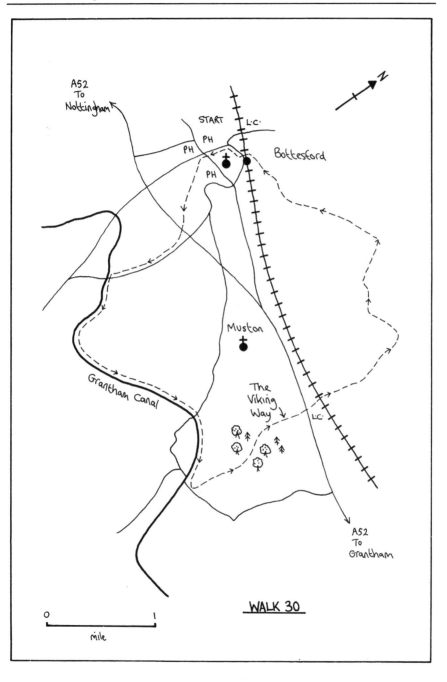

WALK 30

Turn left along the road and you immediately cross the track bed of the Belvoir Branch of the Ironstone Railway that was constructed in 1883 to take iron ore from the Brewers Grave area to the Stanton Ironworks at Ilkeston. At Stenwith Bridge the former Ironstone Railway ran alongside the Grantham Canal to Muston before joining the Nottingham-Grantham Railway line. Prior to the Ironstone Railway Line, iron ore was sent by barge along the Grantham Canal to the River Trent, then the Erewash Canal to reach its destination at the ironworks.

Opposite the Viking Way car park turn left onto a track to join the Viking Way, which follows Lincolnshire's oldest highway. The Sewstern Lane is an ancient drovers route, which was used by packhorses and occasional wagons. Today much of its length forms the boundary between Lincolnshire and Leicestershire. The track is waymarked with the Viking Way motif, and is very pleasant to walk along at the beginning. After noting Breeder Hills Farm to the right, the track becomes rutted and this situation persists until entry into a wood. The track funnels into a woodland path and emerges out by a farmhouse where a farm road is joined for ½ mile to the A52 road again.

Cross the busy road with care to the lane opposite where in 100 yards a level crossing on the Nottingham-Grantham railway line is encountered. If the green light is showing, cross and rejoin the Viking Way now following a farmers track ahead through the flat Lincolnshire countryside. To the left is a wood called The Debdale, and in autumn the colours of the trees are quite spectacular. Bear to the right slightly to join a grassy field track and at a junction of tracks near to Glebe Farm leave the Viking Way and turn left.

With Bottesford church spire in the distance, follow this track for ½ mile, descending a hill to a yellow topped marker post. Turn right along a narrow and perhaps muddy path now back in Leicestershire to a farm track. Turn right and follow this track over two fields to a stream, then turn left along the field perimeter edge for ¾ mile to a hedge gap and clamber over the dyke. Opposite is another hedge gap and from here a very clear field path ascends quite sharply to surprise you with a magnificent panoramic view of Bottesford.

Turn left along a green lane to a level crossing adjacent to Bottesford Railway Station, cross if all clear, and emerge out at a road. Head to the public footpath sign opposite, where a beautiful path traces the course of the River Devon to the left of the church. In due course this will bring you to the entrance gates to the church.

Swans swimming along the Grantham Canal near Muston Bridge

Points of Interest

Bottesford is an attractive village, some 16 miles north of Melton Mowbray, set in the exquisite Vale of Belvoir. The River Devon flows through the village, close the church, and this beautiful corner is a favourite with the local population who enjoy a pleasant seat on a sunny day. The Parish Church of St Mary The Virgin has the highest spire in Leicestershire, 210 feet, which can be seen from many miles around. The church dates from the twelfth century and is often called "The Lady of the Vale". There is a remarkable collection of tombs of the Lords of Belvoir, eight in all, and the tomb of the 6th Earl of Belvoir has an inscription that records the death of two heirs to witchcraft. A visit to the church is a "must" and the holy building will be found open at all times during the day. An excellent guide is on sale inside the church which is worth purchasing.

Muston is a small village dispersed around the church of St John the Baptist. Its best known resident was the poet George Crabbe, Rector from 1789-1814, although he was away from the church for much of the time. He was an unpopular Rector and after the death of his wife, Sarah, he left the village much to the relief of the villagers.

Footnote

Allow a full day for this walk as there is much to digest. The church can be examined either before or after the walk depending on your personal point of view. Personally, I like to get acclimatised first with the local sights before starting to walk.

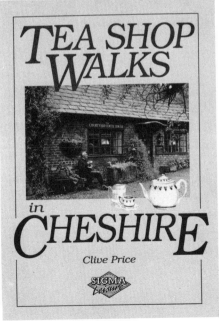